Games of the Orient

PLATE I.　KOREAN OFFICIALS IN MILITARY COURT DRESS.

GAMES OF THE ORIENT

Korea • China • Japan

by

STEWART CULIN

Charles E. Tuttle Company

Rutland, Vermont • Tokyo, Japan

Published by
the Charles E. Tuttle Company
of Rutland, Vermont & Tokyo, Japan
with editorial offices at
15 Edogawa-cho, Bunkyo-ku
Tokyo, Japan

Library of Congress Catalog
Card No. 58-11074

Originally published 1895 by
the University of Pennsylvania, Philadelphia
under the title
Korean Games, with Notes on the Corresponding
Games of China and Japan

Tuttle edition
First printing, 1958

Printed in Japan by
the Mitsumura Printing Company, Tokyo
Color plate by
the Kyodo Printing Company, Ltd., Tokyo

PUBLISHER'S NOTE

First published, by the University of Pennsylvania, in 1895 under the title *Korean Games, with Notes on the Corresponding Games of China and Japan,* this book was from the beginning a collector's item, the original edition being limited to 550 numbered copies. Its author, Stewart Culin, was then Director of the Museum of Archæology and Palæontology at the University of Pennsylvania and a noted collector of games of the world, to which this book serves also as an introduction. With the widespread interest in things Oriental now prevailing in all parts of the Western world, we are happy to be able to provide in this new edition a long unavailable source of information on a particularly charming aspect of the culture of the Far East.

Far from being out of date, it is safe to say that no modern researcher could ever hope to equal the accuracy and scope of Mr. Culin's writing. For in this modern age, when Western influences are transforming so many aspects of the Oriental way of life, introducing new innovations to supersede age-old traditions, many of the games described here have been lost in the welter of postwar change and transition, while others that remain have been so altered as to have lost their true Oriental flavor. Thus Mr. Culin presents a wide range of accurate data on authentic Oriental games and, since a people can often be best understood by their pastimes, also furnishes a valuable insight into the social and ethnological motivations of some of the world's most ancient peoples.

Because the scope of the book is wider than was suggested by its original title, we have adopted what we believe is a more meaningful title. For though Mr. Culin's prime interest was in the games of Korea, his erudite researches and delvings into related games of other Far Eastern countries led him to produce a comprehensive work on Oriental games in general, and the book concerns Japan and China almost as much as it does Korea. In order, however, to retain as much as possible of the quality of the former edition, the text has been reprinted photographically from an original copy of the limited edition of 1895. Of the twenty-two color plates appearing in the first edition, the frontispiece appears here in full color and the others are reproduced in black and white.

CHARLES E. TUTTLE COMPANY

PREFACE.

THIS work is intended not only as a survey of the games of Korea, but as a practical introduction to the study of the games of the world. It is based upon a collection of games made by the writer, and exhibited by him at the Columbian Exposition in Chicago in 1893, and now contained in the Museum of Archæology of the University of Pennsylvania; and upon information obtained from natives of Eastern Asia residing in the United States, the author never having visited the East.

The description of the Korean games was furnished to me orally by Mr. Pak Young Kiu, the accomplished Secretary of the Korean Commission to the Columbian Exposition, and at present *Charge d'affaires* of the Korean government at Washington.

The illustrations are almost entirely by native artists. The Korean plates are faithful copies of part of a series of colored pictures made by Ki San, an artist in the little Korean village of Tcho-ryang, back of Fusan. They represent the people of that locality. They were executed in 1886 upon the order of Miss Shufeldt, daughter of Rear Admiral R. W. Shufeldt, U. S. N., who visited Korea upon the King's repeated invitation just four years after Admiral Shufeldt had negotiated the treaty between Korea and the United States. The sketches in the text are in part by Teotiku Morimoto of Tokyo; in part reproduced from native books, and in part drawn from specimens in the collection of games in the Museum of the University of Pennsylvania.

The incentive to the preparation and publication of this work was primarily the inspiration drawn from suggestions based upon his studies of the institutions and games of primitive American peoples, made to me by my friend and collaborator, Mr. Frank Hamilton Cushing, of the Bureau of American Ethnology, of Washington. In his suggestions as to the object and origin of American games, I recognized a means of removing the study of games and allied customs from the uncertain domain of so-called Folklore into the realm of true scientific investigation. I have left the direct comparison of the games of the two continents to Mr. Cushing, while I have carried forward the investigation of the Asiatic games upon the intrinsic evidence they themselves have afforded.

I desire to express my obligations and thanks to W. H. Wilkinson, Esq., late H. B. M. Acting Consul-General in Seoul, Korea, who placed at my disposal the accounts of Korean chess and playing-cards which are incorporated in this book, and in addition sent me, for the purposes of exhibition and study, his very perfect and unique collection of Chinese playing-cards. I also desire to acknowledge the assistance I have received from many sources in direct contributions of information and gaming material, and in critical suggestions, as well as in perfecting the artistic and mechanical details of this volume. My thanks are especially due to those whose names appear below.

MR. SABURO ARAI, Toyama, Ichigo, Japan.
DR. DANIEL G. BRINTON, Philadelphia.
HON. SIR CHARLES TODD CROSTHWAITE, K. S. I., Calcutta, India.
MR. C. HACHIRO KAJIWARA, Aidzu, Japan.
LIEUT. TATSUZO KOSUGI, I. J. N., Tokyo, Japan.
LI CH'UN SHAN, SINSHANG, Hoh Shan, Kwangtung, China.
MR. BENJAMIN SMITH LYMAN, Philadelphia.
MR. KUMPEI MATSUMOTO, Shidzuoka, Japan.
MR. JUMATSU MATSUO, Nagasaki, Japan.
HON. DATO MELDRUM, Johore, S. S.
MR. KINTARO SATO, Tokyo, Japan.
SYED MOHAMMED HADI, Sultanpur, India.
SWAMEE BHASKARA NAND SARASWATEE, Jodpur, India.
LIEUT. H. L. SCOTT, Third Calvary, U. S. A., Fort Sill, O. T.
COUNT SEYICHIRO TERASHIMA, Kagoshima, Japan.
MR. YASUJIRO YAMAGI, Bingo, Japan.

ARTISTS.

ROBERT G. LEINROTH, Philadelphia.
TEOTIKU MORIMOTO, Tokyo, Japan.
WILLIAM S. RICE, Philadelphia.
WELLS M. SAWYER, Washington, D. C.

MANUFACTURERS.

FRANKLIN PRINTING COMPANY, Philadelphia, Printers.
KETTERLINUS & COMPANY, Philadelphia, Lithographers.
LEVYTYPE COMPANY, Philadelphia, Photo-engravers.

AUTHORITIES CITED.

JOHN D. CHAMPLIN, JR., and ARTHUR E. BOSTWICK, The Young Folks' Cyclopedia of Games and Sports. New York, 1890.

E. J. EITEL, Handbook for the Student of Chinese Buddhism. London, 1870.

EDWARD FALKENER, Games Ancient and Oriental, and how to play them. London, 1892.

DUNCAN FORBES, The History of Chess. London, 1860.

ALICE BERTHA GOMME, The Traditional Games of England, Scotland, and Ireland, Vol. I. London, 1894.

JOHN HENRY GRAY, China. London, 1878.

M. DE GUIGNES, Dictionnaire Chinois, Français et Latin. Paris, 1813.

ANTON HUBER, Über das Meisir genannte Spiel der heidnischen Araber. Leipzig, 1883.

THOMAS HYDE, De Ludus Orientalibus. Oxford, 1694.

JAMES LEGGE, The Sacred Books of China, The Texts of Confucianism, Part II, The Yî King. Part III, The Lî Ki. Oxford, 1882, 1885.

WILLIAM FREDERICK MAYERS, The Chinese Reader's Manual. Shanghai, 1874.

W. H. MEDHURST, English and Chinese Dictionary. Shanghai, 1847.

A. B. MITFORD, Tales of Old Japan. London, 1871.

ROBERT MORRISON, A Dictionary of the Chinese Language. Macao, 1815–1823.

ALBERT NORMAN, Ungdomens Bôk. Stockholm, 1878.

T. A. PURCELL, Our Neighborhood. Yokohama, 1874.

M. L'ABBE DE SAVIGNY, Le Livre des Écoliers. Paris.

Z. VOLPICELLI, Wei-Ch'i, Journal of the China Branch of the Royal Asiatic Society, Vol. XXVI, 1891–92. Shanghai, 1894.

W. H. WILKINSON, A Manual of Chinese Chess. Shanghai, 1893. Chess in Korea, Pall Mall Budget, December 27, 1894. Chinese Origin of Playing-Cards, American Anthropologist, January, 1895.

A. WYLIE, Notes on Chinese Literature. Shanghai, 1867.

WAH KAN SAN SAI DZU E. "Japanese, Chinese, Three Powers (Heaven, Earth, Man), picture collection." Osaka, 1714.

KUN MŌ DZU E TAI SEI. "Very Complete Collection of Pictures to teach the unenlightened." Kiyoto, 1789.

THE JAPANESE MONTHS. Printed by the Kokubunsha, Tokyo.

TRANSLITERATION.

The orthography and transliteration of the Korean words is in accordance with the Dictionnaire Coreen Français, Yokohama, 1880. The Chinese is transliterated in the Canton dialect, following Dr. S. Wells Williams' Tonic Dictionary, Canton, 1856. The Japanese-English Dictionary of Dr. J. C. Hepburn, Tokyo, 1888, has been taken as a standard for Japanese orthography.

STEWART CULIN.

UNIVERSITY OF PENNSYLVANIA,
August, 1895.

PUBLICATIONS ON CHINESE GAMES, BY STEWART CULIN:
Chinese Games with Dice. Philadelphia, 1889.

The Gambling Games of the Chinese in America. Fán t'án: the Game of Repeatedly Spreading Out. Pák kòp piú; or, the Game of White Pigeon Ticket. Philadelphia, 1891.

Chinese Games with Dice and Dominoes. Report of U. S. National Museum, 1893.

Tsz' Fa; or "Word Blossoming." A Lottery among the Chinese in America. Overland Monthly, September, 1894.

CONTENTS.

CONTENTS.

KOREAN PLATES.

FIGURES IN TEXT.

INTRODUCTION.

Therefore, anciently, the son of Heaven chose the feudal lords, the dignitaries who were Great officers, and the officers, from their skill in archery. Archery is the special business of males, and there were added to it the embellishment of ceremonies and music. Hence among the things which may afford the most complete illustration of ceremonials and music, and the frequent performance of which may serve to establish virtue and good conduct, there is nothing equal to archery; and, therefore, the ancient kings paid attention to it.—Li Ki, Book XLIII, Shê I, 4. Legge's Translation, p. 448.

There are two principal questions involved in the study of games : that of their origin, and that of their distribution. Their origin has hitherto generally been vaguely assigned to the inborn tendency of mankind to amuse itself. As lambs frolic on the green, so it is thought man's festal instincts find expression in games and play. The wide geographical distribution of games is accounted for in two ways : by direct transmission from one nation or country to another ; as, for example, the supposed introduction of chess into Europe, and by natural and spontaneous invention under similar influences and conditions. The consideration of the question of origin naturally precedes that of distribution.

Upon comparing the games of civilized people with those of primitive society many points of resemblance are seen to exist, with the principal difference that games occur as amusements or pastimes among civilized men, while among savage and barbarous people they are largely sacred and divinatory. This naturally suggests a sacred and divinatory origin for modern games, a theory, indeed, which finds confirmation in their traditional associations, such as the use of cards in telling fortunes. An examination of the native games of the American Indians throws much light upon the subject. Investigation, however, has been hitherto comparatively unproductive of results, from the fact that most students have failed to perceive the true significance of games in primitive culture, regarding them primarily as pastimes; and, secondly, from their being led by the resemblances between the games of the two hemispheres into the discussion of questions of contact and migration, which have proved unfruitful and inconclusive.

2

Modern games have so nearly lost their original meaning that even with the light afforded by history it is practically impossible to trace their origin. A clue is furnished by America, but there remains a great gap between its primitive conditions and the earliest historic time in Europe, in which games existed as amusements, played in much the same manner, and for the same object as at the present day. Impressed with the difficulties that beset the direct application of the explanations found in primitive life to our own customs, I have turned to Eastern Asia for evidence to connect the remote past with the present, and especially to Korea, a land most prolific in survivals, for confirmation of my theory.

Games, I hold, must be regarded not as conscious inventions, but as survivals from primitive conditions, under which they originated in magical rites, and chiefly as a means of divination. Based upon certain fundamental conceptions of the universe, they are characterized by a certain sameness, if not identity, throughout the world. Without the confirmation of linguistic evidence they are insufficient to establish the connection of races or the transference of culture. They furnish, however, the most perfect existing evidence of the underlying foundation of mythic concepts upon which so much of the fabric of our culture is built, and are of the highest value from the wide application which may be made of the principles which they illustrate.

Before proceeding to discuss the origin of games, I desire to call attention to the remarkable survivals of primitive social conditions that exist in Korea, conditions to which the national games owe their form, if not their very existence. Foremost among them is the division and classification of the people according to the four cardinal points and the middle. This division, common among the American tribes, exists in Korea at the present day. At the age of fifteen years every free-born Korean boy is enrolled by the government, and designated in Seoul as belonging to one of the quarters or the middle. The capital itself is divided into five wards, agreeing with these directions. Again, in the state there are eight provinces,[1] corresponding, it would seem, with the four quarters and the intermediary points. Upon examining the numerical categories of the old Chinese writers and the philosophical systems in which they explain the relations that are supposed to exist between natural phenomena, we find classification, according to the four quarters and the middle, extended not

---

[1] There are 360 magistracies.

only to the regions, but to the seasons of the year, the elements, colors, planets, and the notes of the musical scale.[1] We discover, too, an extension of the system to a nine-fold division of the universe in accordance with the four quarters, the four intermediary points, and the middle, and the classification almost indefinitely extended to every domain of energy and thought. A numerical relation was assumed to exist between the dominant principles with their dependent categories, and the discovery of this relation was believed to furnish a clue to the solution of the profoundest problems of existence.

In this attempt at classification according to the directions which is practically universal among primitive people, things and affairs were encountered which did not in themselves reveal their proper assignment. To effect their classification resort was had to magic. The processes, at first serious and divinatory, afterward practiced as a means of diversion as children play at the serious business of life, became games. The games which thus originated hold a peculiar position among the world's amusements, and may be regarded as games *par excellence*. They frequently retain something of their original character and often survive in two forms, more or less distinct—as a divinatory rite and as a simple amusement.

The study of the games of Korea reveals the fact that there were two principal systems of divination in Eastern Asia, from which games arose, in both of which the arrow or its substitute was employed as the implement of magic. Mr. Cushing has disclosed the importance of the place held by the arrow in primitive culture. It was and is no less significant in Asia than in America. Examining the arrows used in Korea at the present day, they are found to occur in sets of five, each archer usually having three sets. The five arrows are numbered with Chinese characters from one to five. The arrows of each individual bear his name, also written in Chinese characters, and are further distinguished by colored rings as red, green or black on the shaftment, by which the archer more quickly recognizes his

---

[1] The following table, compiled from Part II of Mayer's *Chinese Reader's Manual*, will give some idea of the system of classification as it existed in Eastern Asia:

DIRECTIONS.	SEASONS.	COLORS.	ELEMENTS.	PLANETS.	METALS.	GRAINS.
East,	Spring,	Green,	Wood,	Jupiter,	Lead and Tin,	Corn.
South,	Summer,	Red,	Fire,	Mars,	Copper,	Millet.
West,	Autumn,	White,	Metal,	Venus,	Silver,	Hemp.
North,	Winter,	Black,	Water,	Mercury,	Iron,	Pulse.
Middle,		Yellow,	Earth,	Saturn,	Gold,	Rice.

FIGS. I, II, III.—SHAFTMENTS OF PRACTICE ARROWS, KOREA. UNITED STATES NATIONAL MUSEUM.

own.[1] At an early period in culture the arrow, marked with the designation of its owner, by which he recognized his quarry or the foe that fell before his arm, came to stand as his symbol and representative. From evi-

---

[1] The arrows here referred to are those used in archery. These practice arrows, called *You-yep-tjyen* (Chinese, *lau ip tsin*), or, " willow leaf arrow," are made of bamboo, about thirty-four inches in length. The point is of iron, nail shaped, with a stop which fits against the foreshaft. The latter is usually made of cherry wood with or without the bark on, and is about one and one-quarter inches in length. The footing, also of cherry wood, has a cylindrical nock with a U-shaped notch. The feathers, three in number, are carefully and uniformly trimmed, as shown in Figs. I, II, III, and are fastened with glue, on some in a straight line, and others at a slight angle to the shaft. Some of these arrows in the Museum of the University of Pennsylvania, and in the United States National Museum bear the personal name of the owner, written in Chinese characters between the feathers. On others, in the same collections, the name has been erased in accordance with the sentiment that exists in regard to the personal name. One of these arrows in the National Museum, Fig. II, bears the title of the owner, *Han-ryang* (Chinese, *han léung*), (see pages 62, 64), above the name ; while others in the University Museum is similarly inscribed with *Tchyoul-sin* (Chinese, *ch'ut shan*), the first step in military rank. Many specimens are marked on the foreshaft near the notch with a ring, as Fig. II, or with a black dot, or with both in combination. These are said to be used to distinguish the individual arrows in contests, when for some reason, the personal name is not written upon them. Two arrows in the National Museum, Fig. III, have bands of green paper on the foreshaft. These, with similar ribbons of different colors, are said to be used to enable contestants to readily distinguish their arrows. The last-mentioned arrows have the character *t'ŏ*, " earth," written on one, Fig. III, and *shui*, " water," on the other, on the foreshaft near the notch, instead of rings or dots, and are apparently intended to serve the same purpose.

All of these arrows are numbered with Chinese characters, from one to five, below the fore-shaft. A set consists of five arrows, and in archery contests three sets are usually carried. The suggestion of Mr. Cushing that the Korean card numerals, Fig. 122, are derived from the cut cock-feathers of arrows is not confirmed by the featherings of the practice arrows, which do not appear to be so marked, and to be uniform. It will be observed, too, that the arrows are in sets of five, and do not agree in their numbering with the cards, which are in suites of ten. A miniature quiver with five arrows without points, the whole called *tong-kài* (Chinese, *tsin k'oi*), or " quiver," is carried by high officials in Korea as an emblem of military rank, as is shown in Plate I. The specimen in the United States National Museum, however, has ten instead of five arrows, the feathers of which agree with the feather marks on the backs of the playing-cards, having black tips, which may be perpetuated in the black mark at the top of the scroll on the cards. The corresponding ceremonial quiver in Japan, *yazutsu*, has ten arrows.

In addition to the above-described practice arrows, many other kinds of arrows are used in Korea. The most formidable, which are used in war, are called *hpyen-tjyen* (Chinese, *p'in tsin*), " part arrows." They are much shorter than ordinary arrows, but are shot from the same bow with the aid of a guide or rest. The latter falls when the arrow is discharged, and is recovered by means of a string, by which it is tied to the archer's finger. The specimens in the National Museum are 18 inches in length. They have a heavy conical iron head. The shaftment, which has three feathers, is painted black. These arrows bear no marks and were kept tied in large bundles, to be ready for use when required.

Archery is the test of proficiency in the military examinations in Korea. The candidate shoots five arrows at a mark, and three hits are necessary to qualify, whereby the rank of *Tchyoul-sin* referred to as written on the arrows in the University Museum, is obtained.

dence afforded by the Korean playing-cards it appears that the use of the personal name upon the arrow was preceded by that of the symbol of the world quarter to which the owner belonged. Under these conditions the

FIG. IV.—A SHRINE OF THE GOD OF WAR IN PHILADELPHIA.[1]

arrows of the quivers of the representatives of the quarters stood for the people and the world in its totality. The Korean playing-cards again fur-

---

[1] Cf. *Religious Ceremonies of the Chinese in the Eastern Cities of the United States.* By Stewart Culin. Philadelphia. 1887.

nish the most direct evidence in Asia of the ceremonial use of the arrow in divination, which afterward became an amusement. They still bear representations of the feathers of the arrows from which they were derived, and their Chinese name varies only in tone from that of arrow, *tsin.* The complete pack consists of 80 cards in eight numbered sequences from one to ten, the sequences being designated by symbols which correspond more or less closely with those still assigned to the world quarters.

A simple method of using these numbered arrows survives in the lottery. In Korea numbered balls have been substituted for arrows, but the name of the game, *san-htong* (Chinese, *ts'im t'ung*), betrays its origin. In the Chinese lottery, although written paper lots are employed, they are still 80 in number, and, before playing, gamblers resort to a shrine of the God of War, Fig. IV, and throw 80 numbered arrow lots, Fig. V, to "divine" the lucky numbers.

FIG. V.—TS'IM U IN BOX, TS'IM T'UNG. KWANG-TUNG, CHINA. Museum of Archæology, Univ. of Penna. No. 9,048.

The *rationale* of the lottery, and the similar divinatory processes in which arrows are shaken at random from the lot tube (quiver), is very evident,[1] but the writer is not prepared to offer an explanation of the card

---

[1]As, for example, the Meisir game of the heathen Arabs, in which seven arrows were shaken from a quiver. These arrows may be regarded as probably referring to the seven directions, North, South, East, West, Upper, Lower, and Middle.

The Mei-ir was a game which, from the constant references to it by Arab writers and poets, must have constituted one of the chief amusements of the Arabs before the time of Mohammed. The game was always played in the winter time. The stakes were invariably camels, which were slaughtered and eaten. Marked arrows were used, which were shaken from a holder one at a time by a disinterested third person, and the players won or lost accordingly as the arrows they bet on came out or remained in the holder. The accounts of the game, according to Dr. Anton Huber, to whose learned monograph, *Über das Meisir genannte Spiel der heidnischen Araber,* Leipzig, 1883, I am indebted for the following particulars, are somewhat varied and confusing.

The game was prohibited by Mohammed. In the second year of Higera he uttered a warning

games in which the bundle of arrows, or their substitutes, are mixed (shuffled) and apportioned (dealt) at random among the players.

---

against wine and the Meisir, and two years later he prohibited their use and branded them as the works of the devil.

Huber gives numerous references to the game being played in winter. Not only was there more time to play it at this season, but, as it was the custom to distribute the winnings to the poor, they played it more at this time as the poor were more in need of assistance. The poets before the time of Mohammed always boasted of taking part in the Meisir game, as they got the reputation thereby of being benevolent. It was considered shameful not to take part, and numerous examples are given to show the contempt in which those who declined to participate in the game were held. Such were designated as *baram*, an opprobious word which was only said of those who refrained from the game out of miserliness. A man who fell in battle is praised as one who was not a coward, and would not stay away from the Meisir game when the times were hard. One poet who wanted to outdo others in generosity says to his guests that he is ready to gamble also for horses. The Arabs were such inveterate gamblers they would lose all their possessions, and finally their own person. The players bought amongst themselves the camel to be slaughtered, so that it belonged to them jointly, and the commentary says that this was done on credit, as it was not possible to tell beforehand who was the loser and had to pay. The division of the camel was done by the butcher, who for his trouble received the head and feet. The remainder of the camel was divided into ten parts. Ten or eleven arrows were used, seven of which were marked and won portions of the camel if they were drawn, and three or four, which neither won nor lost and were added to increase the weight or bulk of the arrows. The material of the arrows was the wood of the *nab'a* tree, from which bows also were made. All authorities agree that the arrows were yellow in color. They had a peculiar ring when shaken, so that one could easily distinguish if an arrow of another kind of wood was amongst them.

The first of the winning arrows was called the *Fadd*. It had a single notch in its lower part and when it was drawn it drew one part of the stakes, and when it was not drawn its owner had to pay the price of one part. The second was the *Tau'am*, which drew or lost two parts; the third, the *Rakib*, which drew or lost three parts; the fourth, the *Hils*, which drew or lost four parts; the fifth, the *Nâfiz*, with five parts; the sixth, the *Musbil* or *Musfah*, with six parts, and the seventh, the *Mu'alla*, with seven parts.

The four arrows, which only increase the weight, were called the *Safih*, the *Manih*, the *Muda"af* and the *Wagd*. The number of the winning arrows is everywhere spoken of as seven, but it is reasonable to believe that the additional ones were not always four in number; indeed, according to another authority, they were three instead of four.

The number of the players was not more than seven. If one or two were missing out of that number any of the players could take the surplus arrows. The players took the seven marked arrows according to their circumstances. Thus, if one took the *Fadd*, he won or lost one part of the camel; the *Tau'am*, two parts, and so on. When the number of players was complete the arrows were placed in a piece of leather called the *ribâba*. The one who manipulated the arrows was called the *Hurda*, who was a man well versed in the arrows, and who never ate meat for his pay. Close behind him stood the *Rakib*. As the name signifies, this man had the office of a watcher. A piece of white cloth was spread before the *Hurda*. The *Rakib*, or game overseer, handed the *ribâba* of arrows to the *Hurda*, who seized them with his left hand and put them, with the *ribâba*, under the white cloth and shook them. When one of the arrows projected beyond the others he seized it with his right hand, which was covered with a cloth, and handed it, without looking at it, to the *Rakib*. The latter examined it, and after he had assured himself whether it

A method of divination with the entire bundle of arrows, which is quite intelligible, exists, however, at the present day in Korea, China, and Japan. In this system, called *Eki* (Chinese, *yik*) in Japan, the arrows are primarily employed as magical appliances to ascertain the number, place, or direction, being discovered by counting. The process is a revival of the ancient method of divination which is described at length in the third appendix to the Yih King.[1] It will be seen from the appended note that no very clear idea of the process can be obtained from the Chinese record.

---

was a winning arrow or one of the blank arrows, called *guff*, he would call out to whom it belonged in the first case and what it won. If, on the other hand, the arrow was a *guff* it was immediately replaced in the *ribâba*. When the *Fadd* came out as first arrow its owner received one part and the others continued to play with the remaining arrows for the nine parts of the camel that were left. If the *Tau'am* came after this its owner received two parts and the others continued to play with the remaining arrows for the seven parts. If after these two the *Mu'alla* came its owner received the remaining seven parts. This would close the game, and those whose arrows did not come out had to pay the price of the slaughtered camel. In the above-mentioned case these were the *Rakib*, the *Hils*, the *Nafiz*, and the *Musbil*. These arrows had eighteen parts, therefore the price of the camel was divided into eighteen even shares, and each one shouldered as much of the debt as his winning part would have been of the meat if his arrow had won. The four who lost paid in the proportion of $\frac{3}{18}$, $\frac{4}{18}$, $\frac{5}{18}$, and $\frac{6}{18}$.

If the *Mu'alla* came first, its owner received seven parts of the camel, and all those whose arrows did not come out had to pay, their proportions being $\frac{1}{21}$, $\frac{2}{21}$, $\frac{3}{21}$, $\frac{4}{21}$, $\frac{5}{21}$, and $\frac{6}{21}$. They also had to slaughter another camel, as one of the remaining arrows was the *Musbil*, which drew six parts of the camel when it won, whereas there were only three parts of the meat of the first camel remaining. Those whose arrows lost at the first game were not entitled to eat of the flesh of the first camel. When the second camel was killed, and the *Musbil* came first when the arrows were drawn, its holder received six parts, namely : three parts of the first camel and three parts of the second camel. On the first camel he had to pay $\frac{6}{21}$, but of the second, he had nothing to pay. There remained in this case seven parts of the second camel for which the players continued with the remaining arrows. If the *Nafiz* came, it drew five parts, and its holder had to pay for $\frac{5}{21}$ of the first camel, but nothing on the second. There now remained only two parts of the meat, but one of the remaining arrows was the *Hils*, which could win four parts. It was therefore necessary to kill another camel. Those whose arrows did not win any of the second camel, and they were, if no one re-entered the game, the holders of the *Fadd*, the *Tau'am*, the *Rakib*, and the *Hils*, had to pay for the second camel, in the proportions of $\frac{1}{10}$, $\frac{2}{10}$, $\frac{3}{10}$, and $\frac{4}{10}$ exclusive of their proportion of the first camel. If they killed a third camel and the *Hils* was drawn, its holder receives four parts, viz. : two parts of the second, and two parts of the third camel. There now remained eight parts of the third camel, for which the players continued with the remaining arrows until the arrows came so that their respective winnings were equal with the parts of the meat. It is not clear who had to pay for the third camel if no one re-entered the game, but in the opinion of Dr. Huber, a new camel would be killed only when there was a certainty of there being arrows remaining, which would lose and pay for it.

If pieces remained after all the arrows were drawn, they belonged to the poor of the tribe.

[1] Chapter IX, 49. To heaven belongs (the number) 1; to earth 2; to heaven 3; to earth 4; to heaven 5; to earth 6; to heaven 7; to earth 8; to heaven 9; to earth 10.

As practiced at the present day in Japan, 50 slender, rounded splints of bamboo are employed. These sticks, called *zeichiku* (Chinese, *shai chuk*[1]), Fig. VI, may vary in length from two to fourteen inches. The fortune-teller takes the bundle in his right hand and raises it reverentially to his forehead. He then places the ends in the palm of his left hand and with his right hand shuffles them with a rotary motion, Fig. VII. The bundle is then taken in the right hand, and one splint is placed between the little finger and the third finger of the right hand, Fig. VIII. He then divides the remainder (49) into two parts at random, and places one of the divided bundles between his middle finger and forefinger and the other between his forefinger and thumb. The latter bundle is then counted, two at a time, around the *Pát Kwá*, or "Eight Trigrams," Fig. 81, commencing at the one consisting of unbroken lines, which is designated as *K'in* and corresponds with the North West. The trigram at which the count stops (if there be an uneven number the odd one is not counted) is then noted. A record of

---

50. The numbers belonging to heaven are five, and those belonging to earth are (also) five. The numbers of these two series correspond to each other (in their fixed positions), and each one has another that may be considered its mate. The heavenly numbers amount to 25, and the earthly to 30. The numbers of heaven and earth together amount to 55. It is by these that the changes and transformations are effected, and the spirit-like agencies kept in movement.

51. The numbers of the Great Expansion (multiplied together), make 50, of which (only) 49 are used (in divination). (The stalks representing these) are divided into two heaps to represent the two (emblematic lines, or heaven and earth). One is then taken (from the heap on the right), and placed (between the little finger of the left hand and the next), that there may thus be symbolized the three (powers of heaven, earth, and man). (The heaps on both sides) are manipulated by fours to represent the four seasons; and then the remainders are returned, and placed (between) the two middle fingers of the left hand, to represent the intercalary month. In five years there are two intercalations, and therefore there are two operations; and afterward the whole process is repeated.

52. The numbers required for Khien (or the undivided line) amount to 216; those for Khwăn (or the divided line), to 144. Together they are 360, corresponding to the days of the year.

53. The number produced by the lines in the two parts (of the Yî) amounts to 11,520, corresponding to the number of all things.

54. Therefore by means of the four operations is the Yî completed. It takes 18 changes to form a hexagram.

55. (The formation of) the eight trigrams constitutes the small completion (of the Yî).

56. If we led on the diagrams and extended them, if we prolonged each by the addition of the proper lines, then all the events possibly under the sky might have their representation. *The Sacred Books of China: The Texts of Confucianism.* Translated by James Legge. Part II. *The Yî King*, Oxford, 1882.

[1] *Shai*, "to divine with slips of milfoil; the most efficacious is from the grave of Confucius." *Chuk*, "bamboo."—Williams's *Tonic Dictionary.*

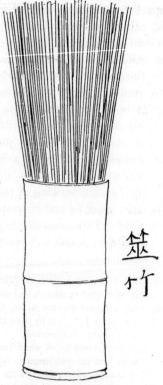

FIG. VI.—ZEICHIKU. DIVINING SPLINTS. JAPAN.

FIG. VII.—SHUFFLING ZEICHIKU. JAPAN.

FIG. VIII.—"ONE SPLINT IS PLACED
BETWEEN LITTLE FINGER."

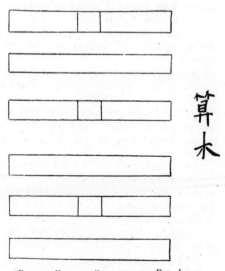

FIG. IX.—FACES OF SANGI USED IN EKI, JAPAN.

this is kept by means of six rectangular wooden prisms called *sangi* (Chinese, *sün muk*), or " calculating sticks," [1] Fig. IX.

These blocks are about four and one-half inches long by three-fourths of an inch square, and have two contiguous sides plain and the other two contiguous sides marked with a square cut across the middle about three-quarters of an inch wide, the depression being painted red. The six *sangi* are laid in a row before the fourtune-teller with the plain faces uppermost. If the lowest line of the trigram at which the count stops is broken, the lowest block of the six, that is the one nearest the diviner, is turned so that the marked side is uppermost. If the lowest line of the trigram is unbroken, the block is allowed to remain in its original position. This is repeated with the second and third blocks, which are arranged to correspond with remaining lines of the trigram. The entire operation is then repeated and the other three blocks turned to correspond with the trigram that is indicated. Reference is then made to the corresponding hexagram in the Yih King, under

FIG. X.—FORTUNE-TELLER WITH ZEICHIKU. JAPAN.
After Purcell.

which is an explanatory text, by means of which, together with traditional interpretations, the augury is made. A knowledge of present events is thus supposed to be obtained, but if it is desired to know the future, the six blocks are reversed, and the result, which is the complement of that first obtained, is referred to the corresponding hexagram.

I am informed by recent travelers in Japan that fortune-tellers with the bundle of splints and a diagram with the Eight Trigrams may still be seen at the street corners.[2] Persons who practice this art, Fig. X, are called *Bai boku sha* (Chinese, *mái puk ché*).

---

[1] Similarly-named sticks are used for performing arithmetical operations in China, Korea, and Japan.

[2] Mitford speaks of the Japanese fortune-tellers " with a treatise on physiognomy laid before

It has been assumed without discussion that the *zeichiku* were originally arrows or arrow shaftments.   Mr. Cushing has clearly demonstrated
the arrow origin of similar objects in America, and additional evidence is
found in China in the name and form of the like implements employed by
the Chinese in an analogous method of divination popularly known from
the name of its reputed inventor *Man Wong* (Wên Wang)[1], as *Man Wong
kwá.*

In this process 64 splints of bamboo, about four inches in length, called
kwá ts'im, Fig. xi, are used.   These splints, which are tipped with red paint,
are marked in four ways: sixteen with a single dot, called *tán*, " single ";
sixteen with two dots, called *chít*, " broken " ; sixteen with a circle, called
ch'ung, " duplicated," and sixteen with a cross, called *káu*, " united."   They
are considered respectively as *yéung*, " masculine "; *yam*, " feminine "; *shiú
yéung* and *shiú yam, shiú* meaning " assistant."   In the practice of fortune-

---

them. . . . If he finds a customer he closes his eyes, and, lifting the divining sticks reverentially
to his forehead, mutters incantations between his teeth.   Then suddenly putting the divining sticks
in two bundles, he prophesies good or evil according to the number in each."—*Tales of Old Japan*,
London, 1871, Vol. I, p. 148.

T. A. P. (Dr. Purcell) in that charming book, *Our Neighborhood; or, Sketches in the Suburbs
of Yedo*, Yokohama, 1874, gives the following account of the Japanese Fortune-Teller: " Having
rattled his rods together by rolling them between his palms, he raises them to his forehead for a
moment in a reverential manner, and then taking one from the bundle lays it on the little table
beside his right hand.   He then proceeds, having divided them into two and rejected one portion,
which he replaces in the pencil-holder, to count out by fours those retained in his hand, and, in
accordance with the broken number left, he moves a block.   This process twice again repeated
by threes on these occasions, and a block moved as before, a combination of the blocks results,
in which the characters upon them correspond with the numbers of a paragraph in a book of
oracular responses, which, when referred to, is accepted as a satisfactory reply to the query.   He
does not, however, depend much upon the book, but trusts in a great measure to his inspiration.
He will tell you that he passes one hour every morning in a religious trance, in which it is revealed
to him what general form of combinations of the *sangi* will be properest for the day.   He professes to know beforehand that certain questions will be asked of him, and is prepared to answer
them accordingly without much deliberation.   Joy or sorrow, anger or dismay, he has found to interfere with the spirit of divination.   He cannot depend upon his prophecies after such emotions."

[1] Si Peh, B. C. 1231–1135.   The chief of the West, the title borne during life by Ch'ang,
Duke of Chow, afterward canonized as *Man Wong,* and recognized as the virtual founder of the
Chow dynasty.   He was hereditary chieftain in the principality of K'i (in the territory of modern
Shensi).   Succeeding to his father's throne in B. C. 1169, the Duke of Chow manifested himself
as a pattern of princely virtues, and was resorted to by multitudes, who eagerly enrolled themselves
among his subjects.   In B. C. 1144 he was denounced by Hu, the *how* or earl of Ts'ung, to Chow
Sin, the debauched tyrant then seated on the throne of the Yin dynasty, as dangerous to the
latter's power, whereupon Chow Sin cast him into prison at Yew Li.   Here during two years he
remained in durance, occupying his leisure in composing an arrangement of the Yih; or, Book of
Changes.—*Chinese Reader's Manual*, No. 570.

telling with these splints the inquirer draws six splints from a vase, and the

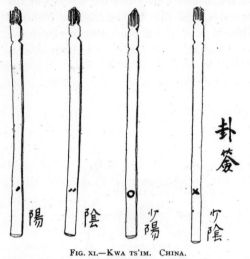

marks upon them are written by the fortune-teller upon paper, that of the first splint drawn being placed at the bottom and the others above, in succession. The six marks are then referred to the hexagram assumed to correspond with them. It will be observed that the *kwá ts'im* have notched points, and their name, *ts'im*, approximates that of arrow, *tsin*.

FIG. XI.—KWA TS'IM. CHINA.

Before considering the other principal method of divination in Asia, out of which games arose, I shall endeavor to indicate some of the most conspicuous survivals of the arrow, as symbolic of man, apart from games in which it was used as his emblem and representative. It is related to me that anciently in Japan the grave of a warrior on the field of battle was marked with his arrow. It is but a step from this custom to the ancestral tablet, and with the latter might be placed the *ho-hpai*, or " name tablet," carried by every male Korean. Direct evidence is lacking in Asia to establish the ancestry I have suggested, but such evidence does exist in the case of a similar and equally significant object, the *p'ái ts'im* or " notice tally," Fig. XII. The Chinese guilds in the United States, when they have occasion to assemble their members, frequently make use of small wooden tablets, bearing on one side the name of the guild, and on the other that of the individual to whom it is sent. These tallies, called *p'ái ts'im*, serve as the credentials of the members at the place of meeting. Their tip, which is painted red, is notched to suggest an arrow, and their name, *ts'im*, the same as that of the preceding splints, approximates that of arrow, *tsin*.

FIG. XII.—P'ÁI TS'IM. NOTICE TALLY. Chinese in Philadelphia.

Fig. XIII represents a carved gambling stick of the Haida Indians, of

Vancouver's Island, B. C., one of a set of thirty-two, bearing devices of the totemic animals of the world quarters, in the United States National Museum. An examination of other sets of Haida gambling sticks shows that this is an elaboration of the sticks marked with colored ribbons, doubt-

FIG. XIII.—HAIDA. INDIAN GAMBLING STICK. U. S. Nat. Museum. No. 73.552.

FIG. XIV.—DEVICE ON HAIDA. INDIAN GAMBLING STICK (BEAVER).

less also having the same significance. Comparing the latter sticks with the arrows of the Northwest Coast Indians, notably those of the McCloud River Indians, of California, it is seen that the banded sticks are directly copied from the arrow shaftments, a complete set representing the arrows of all the people. The Haida gambling sticks may therefore be regarded as the American counterparts of the Korean playing-cards. The latter, from their resemblance to the bamboo lots, *ts'im*, were doubtless originally made of that material. Mr. Wilkinson has referred to the tradition that the devices on the Korean cards were once pictures, more or less carefully drawn, of the various emblems portrayed, and that the present scrawls are declared to be corruptions of these pictures.

FIG. XV.—CYLINDRICAL STAMP. ECUADOR.
Museum of Archæology, Univ. of Penna. No. 12,983.

The carved gambling stick furnishes a suggestion as to the probable origin of the seal cylinder such as was used in ancient Babylonia. Cylindrical stamps of unglazed pottery, pierced with a hole like the seal cylinder of Asia, are found in various parts of America. Such a stamp from Ecuador, Fig. xv, bearing a highly conventionalized device of a bird might readily have been derived from a carved arrow shaftment, and it is reasonable to believe that the Babylonian seals, often bearing devices of animals, and like the carved gambling stick, the emblem and symbol of a man, should have had a similar origin. If we admit this theory of the genesis of the cylindrical seal, may not the flat, carved, wooden seal of Eastern Asia represent the unfolding of the cylindrical seal, and thus be derived through it from the arrow?

A voluminous list might be made of objects of common and general use, among which may be mentioned the folding fan, and in China, the current coin known as "cash," which can be traced with more or less certainty to the marked arrow of primitive culture.

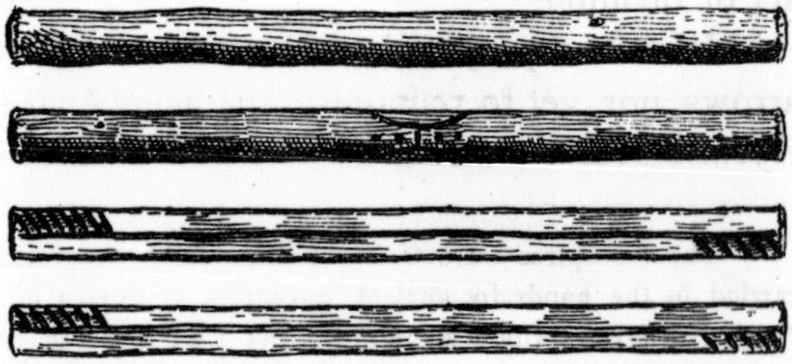

The second method of divination which has given

FIG. XVI.—STAVES USED IN ZOHN AHL. KIOWA INDIANS.

rise to games is one in which several two-faced staves are tossed, and numerical counts attributed to their various falls. Of this, the game of *Nyout* is a striking and typical example.

In *Nyout*, as in many similar games of the same order, direction or place is determined by counting around a diagram which may be regarded as representing the world and its quarters. Such games are found widely distributed throughout the world. In North America they occur in one form or another in almost every tribe, both East and West, and among the Indians of the South-western United States they exist with rules identical with those of *Nyout*, played with four staves upon practically the same diagram. The staves employed in one of these games, the *Zohn Ahl* of the Kiowas, Fig. xvi, enable us, from the arrow marks upon them, to refer the origin of the staves used in America to the arrow. I have indicated on page 73 the probable origin of the *Pát Kwá* or "Eight Trigrams," together with the Sixty-four Hexagrams in the scoring or recording of the falls of two-faced staves. It would appear probable from the American games that these staves were derived from arrows, but the composition of the Chinese character for the name of the diagrams, *kwá*, as well as that for divination by means of the diagrams, *kwá*, does not confirm this. Both are compounded of the character *kwai*, meaning

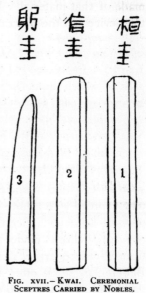

FIG. XVII.—KWAI. CEREMONIAL SCEPTRES CARRIED BY NOBLES. ANCIENT CHINA.

the sceptres anciently carried by nobles, Fig. xvii,[1] one with *puk* "divination" written on the right, and the other with *shau*, "hand," written on the left, the one with "divination" on the right indicating the result or record of the divination, the *kwá*, and the one with "hand" on the left, the act of divining.

I am not prepared to show that these ancient sceptres were originally arrows, nor yet to relinquish the belief that such was the derivation of the *Nyout* staves.[2]

---

[1] These sceptres were of five kinds. They were made of some kind of precious stone and carried in the hands by ancient governors as signals of authority. A duke held an *ún kwai*, "pillar sceptre," which is described as a flat, oblong piece of stone, about nine inches long, rounded at the top and encompassed by a border, Fig. XVII, No. 1. A marquis held a *sun kwai*, "straight sceptre," which is described as resembling the former, about seven inches long, with the border only half round, No. 2. An earl held a *kung kwai*, "crooked sceptre," which is represented as similar to the preceding, also seven inches long, only a little bent, No. 3—. *The Shoo King or the Historical Classic*, p. 18. Translated by W. H. Medhurst, Sen. Shanghai. 1846.

[2] An interesting commentary upon the probable use of the *kwai* or ceremonial sceptre of ancient China in divination may be based upon the so-called mustache sticks of the Ainos of Yezo, Japan. These sticks, which are used to raise the mustache in drinking *sake*, are about fourteen inches

The processes to which I have referred illustrate the two systems of gaming and divination in which the arrow is employed. In the first the entire quiver of arrows (Korean cards, gambling lots) or certain representative arrows (*Meiser*) are used. They are either shaken so that one or more falls according to chance (lottery, *Meiser*) or they are divided at random to ascertain the number (*Eki*) or they are apportioned among the players (cards). In the second the arrows are replaced by two-faced staves, to the falls of which numerical values are attributed. In both systems, when the arrows are used to determine number, a diagram is also used upon which the counts are made, whereby place is ascertained. This diagram, whether the *Nyout* circuit, or the Eight or Sixty-four diagrams, the *Pachisi* cross or the chess-board invariably stands for the world. The cosmical import of game boards is often plainly manifest, but in none more clearly than the Korean board for *Pa-tok*, whose quarters are designated by the cosmical symbols. It is apparent in the divinatory games that the counts refer ultimately to people, and that the counters actually stand for men. In the *Pachisi* game they are differentiated with the colors of the world quarters.

Of the ninety-seven Korean games described in the following pages twenty-three may be referred to the arrow employed as an implement of magic in divination. Among them I have included the Chinese game of dominoes, in which the duplication of the eleven pieces has hitherto remained unaccounted for. Dominoes I now regard as having originated in the attribution of the dice casts to the world quarters, the duplicates being added to complete the circuit of 32, in which each piece has its complement. Hence the cosmical terms, paralleled by those of the Hexagrams, which are given to the pieces. Incidentally, in the consideration of these games an explanation is suggested of the world-wide custom of counting-out among children. The Korean counting-out rhyme will be seen to be a numerical formula, and with the custom of counting around the circuit of the world in divination, in mind, may not counting-out rhymes be survivals of the formulæ used in such counting, applied in counting-out to the representatives of the world quarters? The terms employed in divination in Korea are, as far as

---

in length, flat on one side and slightly rounded on the other, and with one end cut to a point. The rounded face is carved with more or less elaborate designs, which, taken in connection with the scratches on the reverse of the sticks, and the fact that the two faces, as shown by specimens in the United States National Museum, are sometimes lacquered red on one face and black on the other, would seem to bear a cosmical significance, such as may be found in the devices on similar staves used in games among certain of the North American tribes. The mustache sticks would thus appear to form a kind of link, connecting the ceremonial sceptre with the divinatory staves.

I have observed, exclusively of Chinese origin, and a knowledge of their exact meaning is confined to scholars. I cannot leave the subject of these counting games without referring to the explanation of the sinistral and dextral circuits, disclosed to me by a Korean gentleman of rare attainments, whose life had been passed in the study of the Chinese Book of Divination. They represent, he tells me, the Celestial and the Terrestial circuits, one naturally being the reverse of the other.

Ceremonial divination has lost none of the respect in which it was once held in Europe, among the scholars of Korea and China, or even among a few rare students in Japan, who cling to the old order of things. It was an important adjunct of the Chinese art of war, the camp itself being arranged in accordance with the Eight Diagrams.[1] The Korean battle-flags, with the colors of the world quarters and the em-

FIG. XVIII.—SOUL BIRD. ANCIENT EGYPT.

blems of the Four Quadrants, or divisions of the Twenty-eight Constellations,[2] illustrate the harmony that prevails between the symbols of power and the mythic conceptions upon which the theory of the State is founded.

Apart from the games I have considered there remain a large number, consisting in what may be regarded as athletic sports, or in games of children, for which a convenient explanation is found in the festal theory. Some of these games, as wrestling and the fist-game in Japan, which are ceremonially practiced in the pavilions of the Four Directions, and the

---

[1] Chu ko Liang, A. D. 181–234. The great counsellor of Liu Pei invented a formation of troops which he denominated *Pát chan t'ò*, or the tactics of eight lines of battle, which has been the subject of much disquisition —*Chinese Reader's Manual*, No. 88.

[2] 1. The Azure Dragon—on the East. 2. The Sombre Warrior—on the North. 3. The Vermillion Bird—on the South. 4. The White Tiger—on the West.—*Chinese Reader's Manual*, Part II, 91.

divinatory tug-of-war, still retain traces of their primeval divinatory character. In discussing the fist-game with a Japanese adept, he pointed out to me the distinction which should be observed between games and plays. The fist-game as practiced in the pavilion was the true game, while the performance of children and the *Geisha* was only play, they playing or imitating the game, which he regarded seriously. I take it that the plays of children must be regarded apart from games, being dramatic and imitative, although copying games as they copy other affairs of life, and thus often preserving remains of ceremonials of remote antiquity. With children's games may be included their toys, many of which are ceremonial appliances of discarded religions, as the tilting Buddha toy, or remains from that primitive culture which would seem to have been once well-nigh universal.

The kite, with us a mere toy, is seen in Asia to retain suggestions of its original significance as the " over soul," a conception akin to that of the employment of the kite-bird as the emblem of the soul in ancient Egypt.

Games of the Orient

PLATE II.   KOREAN DANCING BOY.

KOREAN GAMES.

I. HTAL-TEUNG.

TOYS AND LANTERNS.

WHEN Korean boys and girls are young they play together, but the better class of people do not permit little girls go out to play with boys. Confucius says that children of both sexes should not sit together when they are seven years of age, and this is observed.[1] When a mother has no milk, rich people have a *you-mo*, or wet nurse, while the *tchim-mo*, or seamstress, makes the baby's clothes. Mothers generally make their own baby clothes, saving the materials before the baby is born, without sewing them.

The first birthday is celebrated at the end of a year, the baby then being considered to be two years old. The parents invite all members of the family, and special cakes are made for the entertainment. A large, round table is covered with hulled rice at this time, upon which various things are placed—a bunch of long yarn, writing materials, paper, pencil and cake of ink, and money. The baby is brought up to this table and all watch very carefully to see which he plays with. If he picks up the bundle of yarn it is thought he will have a long life; if money, that he will be a rich man; or if the writing material, that he will become a prominent scholar. The rice has the same significance as the money. Sometimes the mother or the girls of the family prevent his picking up the rice or money at first, giving him instead the yarn. His birthday is celebrated every year afterward, but not in this way. About this time, or sometimes before, he is given his name for childhood, which he retains until he is fifteen years old, or, in the case of a girl, until she is married.

Babies are sometimes given dried shell-fish to bite on. They have few toys. Their mothers let them take their yarns and reels from their sewing-

---

[1] The sexes are separated at the same age in China, but the custom does not exist in Japan.

3

4

box, but children are not given toys as with us, except once a year. At four or five children commence to go to school and are supposed to be occupied with pencils, paper, and ink. Sewing is the most important thing for girls. Even the children of rich parents must learn to assist the seamstress, so that they will know how to direct their household affairs when they are married.

Once a year the children's festival comes, on the *să-ouel-tcho-hpal-il*, that is the " Fourth month, first eighth day." Toys are universally sold on this day. They are called *htal-teung*, meaning " image lantern," and are of a great variety of forms. Images of birds and beasts are sold in all the markets. Some represent tigers which are ridden by *san-sin* (Chinese, *shán shan*), *i. e.*, " mountain immortals." Horses have *kĭ-săing* or singing girls on their backs. The latter are always represented in these toys as carrying an umbrella, as they always used to carry an umbrella when they went out, not being permitted to ride in a chair with a cover. The tortoise with a rabbit on its back is also a common toy. The story to which it refers has been told by Dr. H. N. Allen in his *Korean Tales*. Another toy is the *ko-yang-i-tjoui*, or " cat and rat," which consists of a small box on the lid of which is a cat that watches a rat which retreats into its hole when the lid is pushed along toward it. A toy which is called the *pek-kouk*, turtle dove, is also sold. This is in the form of a bird with a hole in its back, which is blown into from a tube at the tail and utters the sound of the dove, *pek-kouk !*

The commonest and most popular toy of all is the *Ot-tok-i*, or " Erect standing one." This is an image made of paper, with a rounded bottom filled with clay so that it always stands erect. The figure represents a woman, who sometimes rides upon a tiger.

The eighth day of the fourth month is the day celebrated in Japan as the birthday of Buddha, called there *Kwam butsuye*. It would appear from this that the Korean festival was originally Buddhistic, and probable that the *Ot-tok-i* were once images of Buddha. They may, however, have had a still greater antiquity and been associated with some earlier religious celebration, possibly connected with the Vernal Equinox. In addition to the toys, fire-crackers are also sold, and in the evening there are fire-works throughout the country. Each person has a lantern, which he feeds and keeps alight during the night. It is believed that if its flame burns clearly and steadily it presages a happy and long life. The toy called the *Ot-tok-i*, which has many counterparts throughout the world, may be regarded as a possible survival of the image of a deity which was anciently worshiped in Korea at this season.

In Japan, the "tilting toy," for so this image may be conveniently styled, is made to represent the idol Daruma and receives the name of that personage. It is also called *oki agari koboshi,* "rising up little priest," Fig. 1. In purchasing these toys Japanese boys are careful to buy those that are

FIG. 1.—DARUMA, OR OKI AGARI KOBOSHI. JAPAN.

Museum of Archæology, University of Pennsylvania. No. 7561.

weighted so as to rise up quickly, imperfect ones being regarded as unlucky, the converse also being true.

The *Wa Kan san sai dzu e* has a picture of a toy representing a Buddhist priest, Fig. 2, which is inclined as if to represent a tilting toy.[1] This, with a picture of a toy dog, is described under the heading *Tsuchi ning yo,* or "clay images," with the Chinese equivalents of *nai só yan,* literally "clay-modelled men," and *to yan ying* (another name), "clay images." It relates that the *Sheng fu ron* (Chinese, Ts'ien fú lun), says, "The people of the present day make clay carts and pottery dogs." These, it says, are the clay image of the present day, made by putting clay in molds of human shape—dogs, lions, and monkeys, which are used as children's playthings.

The name *tsuchi ning yo* is applied in Japan to the clay images of men and horses which were anciently buried with the dead to take the place of living sacrifices, and which are now excavated from the ancient sepulchres.

The foregoing would seem to indicate a ceremonial use of the tilting toy in ancient Japan, especially if it should appear that the *tsuchi ning yo* were actually made in this form. However, the sacrificial images from the ancient graves, as shown by original Japanese paintings[2] in the Museum of the University of Pennsylvania, do not appear to have had a rounded base, and the associations of the toy in Japan are entirely Buddhistic

FIG. 2.—TSUCHI NING YO. JAPAN.
From the Wa Kan san sai dzu e.

---

[1] This may be due, however, to an attempt of the artist to show the toy as lying down.
[2] The gift of the Imperial Museum of Japan.

6

The *Bijutsu Sekai*, or "World of Fine Arts,"[1] gives a picture, Fig. 3, of what appears to be a tilting toy, with the English title of "ancient doll." The Japanese text states that it is by Koze Shoseki and represents an ancient earthen idol, *dogu*, the original supposed to be made by Tosaku Kuratsukuri, *Busshi* (maker of Buddhist idols).

In Southern China (Canton) the tilting toy is called *tá pát tò*, "struck not fall," Fig. 4. It is made of stiff paper or card-board painted red, to represent an old man holding a fan. In India, as shown by a specimen sent to the Columbian Exposition in Chicago from the Provincial Museum, Lucknow, this toy is made of paper, and designated as *posti*, or "one addicted to opium."

In France this toy is made to represent a Chinese mandarin, and is called *Le poussah*, Fig. 5. This name is borrowed from the Chinese, being the word *p'ò sát*, a term applied in China to Buddhistic idols. It is the Chinese form of the Sanskrit *Bodhisattva*.

FIG. 3.—DOGU, OR ANCIENT EARTHEN IDOL. JAPAN. From the Bijutsu Sekai.

In Madrid, Spain, it is sold with other children's toys at the annual fair in the autumn. Those purchased by the writer in 1892 represent a monk and a nun, Fig. 6.

In Germany the tilting toy is a common plaything, and is largely manufactured, with other toys for export. It is made in the form of a grotesque human figure, and called *Putzelmann* (South Germany), or *Butzenmann* (North and Central Germany), Fig. 7, a name which has been regarded as meaning about the same as the English "Bogy man."

A more direct etymology has been found in the German *purzel*, "somersault." It is not improbable, however, that the form *butzen* is, as so often happens, a species of popular etymology to connect an originally foreign

打
不
倒

FIG. 4.—TÁ PÁT TO. CANTON, JAPAN. In the author's collection.

[1] No. 6. Tokyo, May, 1891.

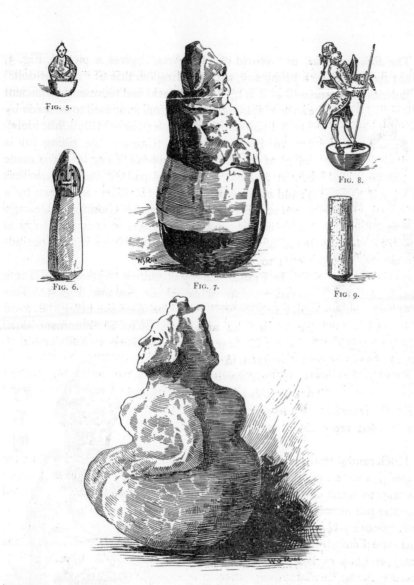

FIG. 10.

FIG. 5.—LE POUSSAH. FRANCE. From *Le Livre des Écoliers*.
FIG. 6.—TILTING TOY. MADRID, SPAIN. Museum of Archæology, Univ. of Penna. No. 16,100.
FIG. 7.—PUTZELMANN. GERMANY. (Made in Paris, France.) Museum of Archæology, Univ. of Penna. No. 18,309.
FIG. 8.—TROLLGUBBE. SWEDEN. From *Ungdomens Bok*. Stockhölm, 1878.
FIG. 9.—TILT-UP. UNITED STATES.
FIG. 10.—CEREMONIAL POTTERY VASE. Grave in Southeastern Missouri. Museum of Archæology, Univ. of Penna. No. 11,589.

word with one already existing in the language and resembling the borrowed word in sound. In view of the difficulties encountered by Germanic scholars in satisfactorily accounting for the name of the toy, the question suggests itself whether it is not an altered and corrupt form of Buddha, as is directly apparent in the French name.

In Sweden this toy is called *Trollgubbe*, Fig. 8, or "old goblin."

Tilting toys of a variety of forms are sold at present in the United States. They are chiefly of foreign manufacture and are known by various names. In Maryland they were formerly called "Bouncing Betty," and in Philadelphia, some thirty years ago, "Bouncing Billy." A miniature tilting toy, Fig. 9, was common in the United States at about the same time, and locally known as a "tilt-up."

Objects of stone and pottery simulating a human figure and having a rounded base like the *Ot-tok-i*, are found widely distributed among the Indian tribes of the United States, by whom they were used in ceremonials and as objects connected with worship. A striking example of such an image is represented in Fig. 10—a vase of painted pottery from an Indian grave in Southeastern Missouri, collected by Mr. Horatio N. Rust. It forms one of a series of similar objects in the University Museum, the evolution of which can be traced clearly from the gourd vessel imitated in pottery, by the aid of examples in the same collection.

II. NOUN-MI-RYEK—SNOW-MAN.

Skates and sleds are unknown as playthings in Korea, although they are used by hunters in the north. Boys slide on the ice, and a favorite winter amusement is to build a snow-man. The "snow-man" is called *Noun-mi-ryek*, or "snow" *mi-ryek*. *Mi-ryek*, for which the *Dictionnaire Coréen Français* gives the Chinese equivalent of *shik yan*, or "stone man," is the name applied to the standing stones which occur in various parts of the country, the largest being known as the *Eun-tyin mi-ryek* from the little town near Seoul, in *Koa-tchyen*, where it is located.

In Japan, boys commonly make a snow-man in the form of the idol Daruma. They frequently hollow out the interior of the image to form a snow-house.

Snow-shoes, *Syel-măl*,[1] "snow horses," are used in the country in hunting, as represented in Plate III. They are of great antiquity in Korea, according to my informant, but are not used by boys in their sports. Stilts

---

[1] Chinese, *süĕ mă*.

군 양 사 눈 머 셜

PLATE III.   KOREAN HUNTERS ON SNOW SHOES.

were introduced into Korea from Japan within the last ten years, but are not much used at the present time. They are called *Take uma*, " bamboo horses," in Japan, Fig. 11.

III. KAK-SI-NO-REUM—DOLL PLAY.

Little girls make their own dolls. They cut a bamboo pipe-stem about five inches long, into the top of which they put long grass, which they have salted and made soft, and fix like the hair of women. No face is made, but they sometimes paste a little white powder in its place. They dress the stick in clothes like those worn by women, and sometimes put a hair-pin, which they make themselves, in the hair.

IV. KEU-RIM-TJA—PICTURES' SONS, *i. e.*, SHADOWS.

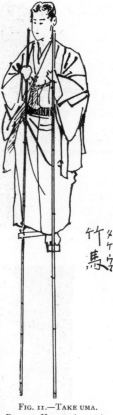

竹馬
ケ
タ
ウ
マ

FIG. 11.—TAKE UMA.
BAMBOO HORSES (STILTS)
JAPAN.

Shadow-pictures are made on the wall with the hand. They are always intended to represent a priest of Buddha, *tjoung* (Chinese, *sang*). A piece of paper, bent in a certain manner, is placed upon the back of the bent hand to form the head and cap of the shadow, while the little fingers and thumb represent the arms. The shadow figure is made to dance in the manner of the priests at certain ceremonies.

Shadow-pictures are also made on the wall with the hand in Japan, where they are called *kage ye*, literally " shadow-pictures." The commonest one is that of the *tori sashi*, Fig. 12, " a person who catches birds with a pole armed with bird-lime." [1] A piece of paper bent in a triangular shape is put on the back of the bent hand to form his hat, as in Korea. He brandishes a pole with which he is supposed to catch birds. Shadow-pictures are likewise made in Japan by means of small figures cut in black paper and mounted on sticks, Fig. 13. These are also called *suki ye* " (light) passing through pictures."

V. NYEN—KITES.

Koreans attribute the invention of the kite to a general in the war with Japan four hundred years ago. His soldiers were dispirited by reverses,

[1] Hepburn.

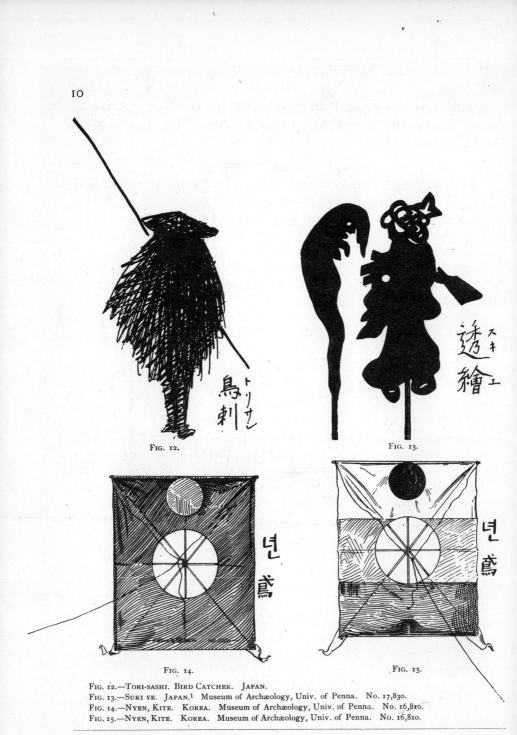

FIG. 12.

FIG. 13.

FIG. 14.

FIG. 15.

FIG. 12.—TORI-SASHI. BIRD CATCHER. JAPAN.
FIG. 13.—SUKI YE. JAPAN.[1] Museum of Archæology, Univ. of Penna. No. 17,830.
FIG. 14.—NYEN, KITE. KOREA. Museum of Archæology, Univ. of Penna. No. 16,810.
FIG. 15.—NYEN, KITE. KOREA. Museum of Archæology, Univ. of Penna. No. 16,810.

[1] The figure on the left represents a *yŭrei*, or " ghost," who appears as a woman with disheveled hair hanging over her face.

연날 는아회

PLATE IV.　KOREAN KITE FLYING.

and at last altogether discouraged by the appearance of falling stars in the sky. He then made a kite, to which he attached a small lantern, and sent it up on a dark night. The soldiers accepted the appearance of the light, which seemed like a new star, as an auspicious omen, and renewed the struggle with increased energy. Another story is told of a Korean general who bridged an otherwise impassable stream by flying a kite which lodged in a tree. He pulled a strong cord across by means of the kite string, and continued the process until a bridge was constructed upon which he and his army passed in safety.

Korean kites are rectangular in form and made with a bamboo frame covered with strong paper, having a circular hole in the middle. They are distinguished by their colors and by a disc of colored paper called the *kkok-tji*, which is pasted upon the face of the kite above the middle. They also have a triangular piece of white paper, called *kal-ka-pal*, or "crow's foot," pasted at each of the lower corners. These are now made quite short, but are said to have been formerly much longer, but to have been diminished in size as a matter of convenience in kite fighting.

The *kkok-tji* are of different colors. The body of the kite is sometimes made of one color, or of bands of different colors. One having bands of three colors is spoken of as *sam-tong-tchi-ma* (Chinese, *sám tung kw'an*), literally "three-colored skirt" or "robe." (*sam-tong*, "three united;" *tchi-ma*, a "woman's robe.") A kite ornamented with a number of transverse bands of different colors is called *hpal-koai-nyen*, or "eight diagram kite."

Kites are said to be of different sizes. They are made by professional kite-makers and cost about ten cents of our money for the best kinds. The kite string, *nyen-tjoul*, is made of pure silk, sometimes colored, that used in the royal palace being sky-blue. The string is the most expensive part, and many men save money during the year to buy kites and string at the appropriate season. The string is wound around a reel of unpainted wood called *el-lai*.

The Korean kites in the Museum of Archæology of the University of Pennsylvania, which were obtained through the courtesy of His Majesty's Commissioner at the Columbian Exposition, are uniform in size, seventeen inches by twenty inches, with a hole in the middle eight inches in diameter. One, Fig. 14, is of blue paper, with a crimson *kkok-tji*, and another, Fig. 15, of yellow, red, and green (*sam-tong-tchi-ma*), with a black *kkok-tji*. A third, which is not figured, has transverse stripes of pink, blue, yellow, red, light-green, drab, and dark-green (*hpal-koai-nyen*), with a black *kkok-tji*.

The Korean kite reel in the Museum of the University, Fig. 16, is about thirty-one inches in length and is wrapped with silk string of four colors—white, green, red, and yellow.

It is customary for all classes in Korea from His Majesty, the King, down, to fly kites. Women sometimes fly kites from their yards, but it is said that any one can tell when a kite is flown by a woman. The owner of a kite is often considered unable to fly it, and when he goes away, another who understands kite-flying will take the reel and play it.

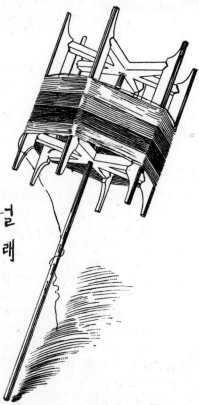

FIG. 16.—EL-LAI, KITE REEL. KOREA.
Museum of Archæology, Univ. of Penna. No. 16,809.

The Koreans say that the Chinese do not know how to fly kites, and that when a Chinaman grows tired after having sent up his kite with a heavy string, he will tie it to a tree and lie down and watch it.

The time for kite-flying is the first half of the first month. After this time, if any one should fly a kite he would be laughed at, nor will any one touch a lost kite.

On the fourteenth of the first month it is customary to write in Korean characters on kites a wish to the effect that the year's misfortunes may be carried away with them. Mothers write this for their child, with his name and the date of his birth. The letters are placed along the bamboo frames so that they may not be seen by any one who might be tempted to pick the kite up. Boys tie a piece of sulphur paper on the string of such a kite, which they light before sending it up, so that when the kite goes in the air the string will burn through and the kite fall.

The Korean name for kite, *nyen*, is apparently the Chinese *ün*, a kite or fish-hawk, the character for this bird being given as the Chinese equivalent for *nyen* in the *Dictionnaire Coréen Français*.

The significance of the kite in Korea is clearly suggested in its use as a scapegoat. It may be considered as the "flying one," represented by the kite bird, the flyer *par excellence.* Kites are described in the *Wa Kan san sai dzu e,* under the name of *ika nobori,* Fig. 17, and *kami tobi* (Chinese, *chi chi*), "paper hawk." It also gives as names *fu sho* (Chinese, *fung chang*), "wind harp" (referring to the singing kite), and *she ro she* (Chinese, *chi lò ch'i*), "paper owl." It states that at the present day, *i. e.,* the time of its publication, A. D. 1712, kites are called *ika* (Chinese, *ü ts'ák*), "cuttlefish," and in the eastern part of Japan *tako* (Chinese, *cheung ü*), the octopus. The same book quotes the following story of their origin from the *Ji butsu ki gen* (Sz' wuh kí yuen): "When Kao Tsu[1] chastised Chin Hé, Han Sin[2]

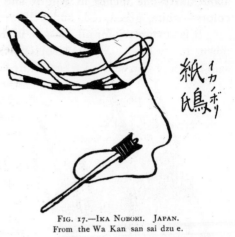

FIG. 17.—IKA NOBORI. JAPAN.
From the Wa Kan san sai dzu e.

planned to come out in the midst and made a kite and sent it up to measure the distance of the palace, desiring to dig a tunnel to enter into the middle of the palace. This is the tradition which is handed down from ancient times."

Kites are popularly known at the present day in Japan as *tako,* "octopus," or *ika,* "cuttlefish." A great variety of forms occur, which receive special names.

In Nagasaki, the kite commonly used in kite fighting is called *hata,* "flag," Fig. 18. It is nearly square, and has two strings attached, one midway above the centre and the other at the lowest corner, as shown in the figure. It is generally

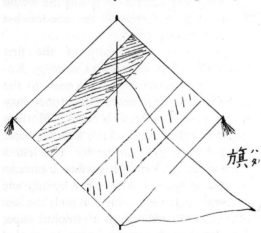

FIG. 18.—HATA. FLAG KITE. NAGASAKI, JAPAN.

---

[1] The founder of the Han Dynasty, died, B. C. 195. *Chinese Reader's Manual,* No. 414.

[2] A general who commanded the armies of Liu Pang who afterward reigned as Kao Tsu. Died B. C. 196. *Ibid.,* No. 156.

ornamented with bands of red, white, and blue, like the Dutch flag, from which its name of *hata*, "flag," is said to be derived.

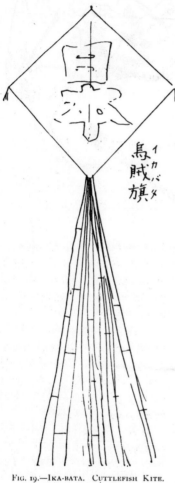

The kite used by children in Nagasaki, called *ika-bata* (*hata*), or "cuttlefish kite," is represented in Fig. 19. It differs from the preceding, *hata*, in its tail, *shippo*,[1] which is made of lengths of white paper about twelve inches long. Three or four of these are pasted end to end, and a bundle of the strips tied at the bottom of the kite, giving it the appearance of a cuttlefish. The strings are fastened in the same manner as on the *hata*. The frame of both of these kites is made of two strips of bamboo placed at right angles. The *hata* has a connecting cord around the edge, which is lacking in the *ika-bata*.

In the provinces of Suruga and Totōmi the kites used in kite fighting are called *buka*. They are rectangular in form, and are sometimes pointed at the bottom, when they are called *tongari*, or "pointed" *buka*. They are always very light in color.

The kite commonly used by boys in Tokyo is rectangular in form and is commonly known as *tako*. It is usually ornamented with a picture, a common device being a stork and tortoise, the stork being represented in white on a crimson ground, and the tortoise in blue water. A picture of Shoki (Chinese, Chung Kw'ei),[2] is another favorite emblem upon kites at Tokyo, Fig. 20.

FIG. 19.—IKA-BATA. CUTTLEFISH KITE. NAGASAKI, JAPAN.

In addition to the simple forms, a variety of fanciful kites are common

---

[1] The name given to the tails of birds and animals.

[2] Chung Kw'ei, the "Demon Queller," a favorite myth of the Chinese, was supposed to be a ghostly protector of the Emperor Ming Hwang (A. D. 713–762). He is usually represented a burly, truculent giant clad in official garb and armed with a two-edged sword. He is commonly shown as punishing or compelling to menial service a band of pigmy demons who adopt the most comical subterfuges to escape from the keen eye of their persecutor.

in Japan. Children fly kites in the form of birds, and both at Tokyo and and Nagasaki, a kite called *yakko-bata*, or "servant kite," Fig. 21, is extremely popular.

At Nagasaki a favorite kite is known as the *tsuru kame*, or "stork and tortoise" kite, Fig. 22. Another is the *ogi no jigami*, or "fan-paper" kite, Fig. 23. The latter is sometimes made to represent a "double fan," *kasane ogi*, Fig. 24. Children in Nagasaki fly a kite known as *oni-dako (tako)*, or "Devil kite," Fig. 25. This bears a picture of the head of the famous warrior Raiko, surmounted with the head of an *oni*, or "devil," referring to a well-known story.[1]

The Chinese at Nagasaki have different kites from those used by the Japanese. The shapes of their kites are even more varied. Birds and centipedes and ·representations

FIG. 20.—SHOKI KITE. TOKYO, JAPAN.

of men, Fig. 26, are common.

FIG. 21.—YAKKO-BATA. SERVANT KITE. JAPAN.

The frames (*hata no hone*, "bones of kite,") of Japanese kites are always made of bamboo. They are invariably covered with paper at the present day. The strings, *itome* (Chinese, *sz' muk*), "string eye," are made of hemp. Reels, *itomaki*, are commonly used. The size of a kite is usually estimated by the number of sheets of paper

[1] *Oe yama oni taiji*, "The *Oe* Mountain Devil-Destroying."

used in its construction, as for example, *juni mai no tako*, a "kite of twelve sheets."

It is customary to attach a "hummer," *unari*, to large kites. This is

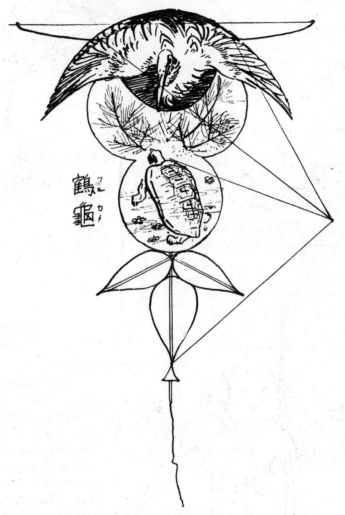

鶴亀

FIG. 22.—TSURU KAME. STORK AND TORTOISE KITE. NAGASAKI, JAPAN.

fastened to the top of the kite, as shown in Figs. 22, 23, 24, and consists of a bow of bamboo with a cord of raw-hide. Boys are extremely proud of the noise made by their kites. At Nagasaki, kites having such a hummer attached are called *bara-mon*.

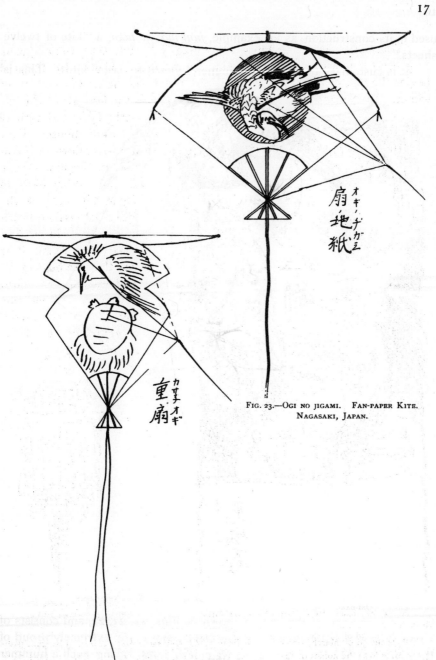

扇
地
紙
_オ_ギ_ノ_ヂ_カ_ミ

重
扇
_カ_サ_ネ_オ_ギ

FIG. 23.—OGI NO JIGAMI.   FAN-PAPER KITE.
NAGASAKI, JAPAN.

FIG. 24.—KASANE OGI.   DOUBLE FAN KITE. NAGASAKI, JAPAN.

The season for flying kites varies greatly in different parts of Japan. In general it appears to depend upon the prevailing winds. In Tokyo it begins the first of the first month. Kites are never flown in summer or winter. In Nagasaki the days for kite flying are the festivals of the 3d,[1] 10th, 15th, and 25th of the third month. They are never flown in Nagasaki in the first month. In some other parts of Japan the 5th[2] of the fifth month is the especial time of kites. In the province of Suruga, it is said that the boys in all families that can afford it have a kite on this day. It is considered very unlucky here for a

FIG. 25.—ONI-DAKO. DEVIL KITE. NAGASAKI, JAPAN

FIG. 26.—CHINESE KITE. NAGASAKI, JAPAN.

[1] "On the 3d of March, which is a holiday called *Jōmi no sechiye* (*sechiye*, 'a banquet given by the Mikado to the nobles of the court,' a 'feast;' *no* 'of;' *Jōmi*, the cyclical name of the 3d of the third month). In houses where there is a little girl of less than seven years of age, there is a pretty display of dolls and small figures, called *Hina no matsuri* (*matsuri*, 'religious festival;' *no*

boy to lose his kite. It is related that a boy once lost his kite upon the day of this festival. A few months later, the boy died. It is customary for search parties to follow a lost kite, sometimes for a distance even of twenty miles. Those who bring back such a kite are given an entertainment, and rewarded with presents of *sahe*.

From this custom, the kite would appear here to be regarded as the emblem of one of the personalities of the boy. Girls never have kites.

In Nagasaki, when a kite escapes, no special effort is made to recover it.

Many stories are current in Japan in which kites figure. Among others, it is related that Ui Shosetsu, who tried to overthrow the Tokugawa government in the seventeenth century, made a large kite on which he

---

' of;' *hina*, 'dolls,' literally ' chickens,' or ' young birds '). These figures, which are dressed to represent the costumes of former days, are arranged in tiers, figures of the Emperor and Empress being given the highest place, while below them, in succeeding ranks, are warriors, court ladies, musicians, etc. At the bottom are arranged little models of the articles necessary for a bride going to the house of a husband—chest of drawers (*tansu*), long box for bed-clothing (*nagamochi*), towel-horse (*iko*), mirror on stand, and so forth. The large dolls ordinarily used for playing with form a part of the show, as does also a model of the small carriage, drawn by oxen, which was used by the Emperors in former days. Large diamond-shaped cakes, called *kusa-mochi*, made of rice and boiled mugwort, are offered to the figures, and are given to those friends and relatives who presented the dolls. The origin of this is not known, but it is supposed to date from over 900 years ago."—*The Japanese Months*, Vol. I. March.

[2] " The 5th of May is marked by a festival called *Tango no sekku* (*sekku*, 'holiday;' *no* ' of;' *tango*, the cyclical name of the 5th of the fifth month), in honor of boys, the girls already having had their day, on the 3d of March. It is celebrated in every house which has been favored with the advent of a boy baby during the previous twelve months, and, to a less extent, in houses where there are boys below the age of seven. In front of the door are set up flags bearing the family crest, figures of warriors, elephants, tigers, dragons, and so forth. The most conspicuous object, however, is a tall pole, generally surrounded by a round basket, covered with gilding, and having attached to it long narrow streamers, and a little wheel turned by the wind. From these poles, bellying out in the breeze, are one, or two, or three larged-sized colored carp, made of cloth or paper. The carp being a fish which resolutely overcomes all the difficulties it encounters in its passage up the streams of the country, even ascending waterfalls, and eventually, it is said, being changed into a flying dragon, it is chosen to shadow forth what it is hoped will be the career of any youthful male members of the household. Inside the house, small flags and a military ensign, *umajirushi*, are set up in a wooden frame, together with helmets, and figures of fighting men, all being expressions of the hope that the small boys of the house may ultimately become great men. Old books say that this holiday was observed as far back as the reign of Jintoku Tenno, about fifteen centuries ago."—*The Japanese Months*, Vol. I. May.

There appears to be a more or less intimate association between the long flags, *nobori*, the carp, *koi*, made of cloth or paper, *koi nobori*, and kites, which are designated, as seen in the *Wa Kan san sai dzu e*, as *ika nobori*. They are all connected with the boys' festival, on the 5th of the fifth month. *Nobori* means literally " to go up, to ascend."

ascended to overlook the castle of Yedo. It is also told that the famous robber, Ishikawa Goemon, in the sixteenth century, attempted to steal the gold from the celebrated golden fish on the Castle of Nagoya by mounting on a kite. Since that time, it is said that large kites are prohibited in Owari.

VI. NYEN-E-OUL-NI-KI—KITE FIGHTING.

Simple kite flying, *nyen-nol-i-ki*, or " kite playing," is quite secondary in Korea to the sport of kite fighting, *nyen-e-oul-ni-ki*, that is, " kite uniting," or " bringing together." Kite flying is practiced chiefly with this in view, the silk strings being prepared their entire length by dipping them in fish-glue to which some sharp material, such as powdered glass or porcelain, has been added. Any kite, no matter to whom it belongs, may be cut down by another. The moment two kite-strings are crossed, the players must let out their lines, as when one of them becomes tense, it is immediately cut through. Sometimes four or five strings are crossed, and the sport often lasts all day. The moment a kite is cut down it is at once seized by small boys who watch for such catastrophies. It is a common saying that there is no property in a lost kite, and when a kite is cut all of the string that may be off the reel is also forfeited. Kites are not matched by previous arrangement in Korea, and their owners do not bet upon them. Hummers are not put in kites, as in Japan. Silk string, which is sold by weight, is invariably used, except by young boys, who have cotton cord. All silk string is first prepared with glue, and fresh glue put upon it, to which the glass or porcelain is added, when it is used.

From the preceding account of kites in Japan, it is natural to suppose that kite fighting is not as general or as popular in Japan as in Korea. It is, however, very common, being called *tako no kiri-ai,* or " kite cutting." [1] Powdered glass or porcelain is fastened to the line with rice-paste for about a hundred fathoms below the kite, and sometimes a sharp, curved knife-blade is attached, in order to cut another's cord. Men frequently match their kites by appointment. At Nagasaki, kite fighting is one of the favorite sports among men, who wager much money on their kites. In Suruga, kite fighting would appear less popular. A secret enemy will sometimes attempt to cut down another's kite, and boys are generally careful not to entangle their kite-strings. When such entanglement happens, they frequently come to blows.

---

[1] In Nagasaki it is called *kakeko suru.*

PLATE V. KOREAN ROPE WALKING.

VII. EL-NENG-TJIL.

When boys secure the string of a lost kite, they frequently tie stones to pieces of the string, and fight them by whirling the stones so that the strings cross and cut each other, in somewhat the same manner as when attached to the kites in the air. This is called *el-neng-tjil*.

VIII. SYOK-KOP-TJIL-HA-KI —PLAYING HOUSE.

Little girls in Korea play house in much the same manner as children do in Europe and America. They have no specially

FIG. 27.—MAME NING YO. BEAN DOLL. JAPAN.

made toys for the purpose, but use clam-shells and small cups from the table service, in which they pretend to serve food. Little girls in Japan play house, using sea-shells and toy utensils, of which a great variety are sold. They call it *mama goto*, "rice (repast) play."

IX. KOANG-TAI—ROPE-WALKER TOY.

Boys make a toy of paper imitating a *koăng-tăi*, or "rope-walker," which they call by that name. Small stones are tied to the legs, which are placed astride a cord, along which the figure is made to move by striking the cord on the side toward which it is desired to go. They sometimes whistle through a crook in their little finger when they play with this toy. A similar toy is made in Japan, under the name of *mame ning yo*, or "bean doll," Fig. 27. Its arms are represented by a cross-piece of bamboo, to the ends of which beans are attached. It is usually balanced on the finger.

FIG. 28.—TSUNA-WATARI. ROPE-WALKING. From the Wak Kan san saí dzu e.

X. TO-REU-RAK-I—WIND-MILL.

Children make wind-mills of paper with two vanes which represent kites (v). The shape is always the same, but the color varies, and they frequently have a picture of a man on one vane and a woman on the other. In Japan, the wind-mill is a common toy, and is made of paper vanes fastened on slips of bamboo, which are arranged like the spokes of a wheel.

The vanes are usually alternately red and white, or other colors. It is commonly called *kazaguruma* (wind-mill), and sometimes *hana-garuma* (flower-mill), the latter name being applied to a special kind.

XI. SEU-RAM-I—THE BUZZ.

This receives its name from the sound it makes. There are two kinds: one a simple circular card, with two holes through which

FIG. 29.—BUN BUN. BUZZ. JAPAN.
Museum of Archæology, University of Penna. No. 16,219.

cords are passed, and the other a tube of bamboo, which is held vertically, within which is an axle terminating in a kind of vane of different colored paper, which is made to revolve by means of a string which wraps and un-wraps itself about the axle. In Japan, a buzz called *b u n b u n*[1] is made out of a rec-tangular slip of bam-boo, Fig. 29, about two and o n e - h a l f inches long, through which two cords are passed.

The buzz is to be found widely distribu-ted among the In-dians of North Ame-rica. Fig. 30 repre-

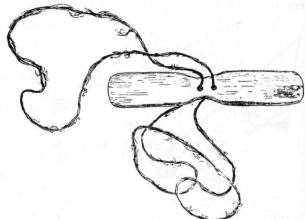

FIG. 30.—BUZZ. NORTH GREENLAND ESKIMO.
Museum of Archæology, Univ. of Penna. No. 18,391.

sents a buzz made of ivory, with a cord of sinew from the North Greenland Eskimo, collected by Mr. Henry G. Bryant. The second form[2] is common

---

[1] This name, which is evidently imitative of the sound of the buzz, was given me as its vulgar name, and its more technical name, if it possesses one, is unknown to me.

[2] This is also common in India. A specimen from Lucknow, called *charki*, is made of tin.

in Japan, under the name of *Tombo*, or "dragon fly," a name which is also given to the flying toy, Fig. 31, made by affixing a rectangular strip of bamboo, cut in a slightly twisted or screw-like shape to the end of a stick which passes through it. In China (Canton) a buzz is made out of a disc of wood pierced with two holes, like the first-mentioned Korean form, or, the seed-pod of the *ling kok* (*Trapa bicornis*) is hollowed out, and cords passed through it. These toys are called *máng fung ché*, "pulling wind-wheel."

FIG. 31.—TOMBO. DRAGON FLY TOY. JAPAN.
Museum of Arch., Univ. of Penna. No. 16,225.

XII. TJOUK-PANG-OUL (DEVIL ON TWO STICKS, *Diable*).

Jugglers, *syot-tai-hpăi*, who travel about the country in large parties, play with an object made of two inverted cones fastened together at the apex, and manipulated by means of a cord, which is attached to two sticks, one of which is held in either hand. Champlin and Bostwick[1] give the following history of a toy similar to the above, under the name of "Flying Cone," or "Devil on Two Sticks," Fig. 32. "This toy had its origin in China, where peddlers use it to announce their approach by its humming. The Chinese form is much larger than ours, and consists of two cylinders of metal or bamboo, united by a thin stem. A string makes a running knot around the stem, and no sticks are used in spinning it. On its introduction into Europe, early in this century, it assumed its present form. In France, where it is called *le diable*, it was at one time so popular that, says a French writer, the toys were made of the most valuable

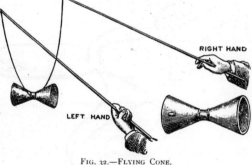

RIGHT HAND

LEFT HAND

FIG. 32.—FLYING CONE.
From *The Young Folks Cyclopædia of Games and Sports*.[2]

---

[1] *The Young Folks' Cyclopedia of Games and Sports*, New York, 1890.
[2] With courteous permission of Messrs. Henry Holt & Co.

woods, and even of glass. They were played with in parlors and on roofs, in public places, and promenades; the sport was not confined to children, but ladies and even persons of eminence strove to excel in it."

XIII. HPAING-I—TOPS.

Tops are played in winter on the frozen ground, being spun with a whip. There are no particular games. They sometimes have iron points, and are made of a hard wood, called *tan-mok*.[1] The ironing sticks are also made of this wood, and their makers cut the pieces from the ends into tops. This wood is from the tree under which it is said the first king of Korea sat when he came from heaven. His Majesty the King of Korea is therefore called *Tan-Koun* from the name of this tree. The *Dictionnaire Coréean Français* also gives *Hpạing-keu-ram* as a little top, which is turned with the forefinger and thumb, an amusement of children. It defines *hpạing* as an imitation of the sound made by a stone in the air, of a ball, or of the top of children.

My Korean informant tells me that tops are also called *hpạing-ko*. Plate VI. represents country boys whipping tops on the ice.

Top-play is described under two titles in the *Wa Kan san sai dzu e*. One, *koma* (Chinese, *tuk lok*) "solitary pleasure," Fig. 33, and the other *bai mawashi* (Chinese, *hoi lo lung*), or "conch-shell play," Fig. 34.

The writer says he considers the *koma* as different from the *bai mawashi*, Fig. 35, although the amusement is the same. The latter is played by a number of persons as a gambling game, observing gains and losses, while the *koma* is not used for gambling; hence the name "solitary or individual pleasure."

In modern times we have the *chikujen hakata*[2]*-goma*, which is made of wood, in the form of a lotus seed-pod, the size of a fist, Fig. 36. The spindle is made of iron like a nail, which is wrapped with cord that is pulled around. It prevailed during the *Gen Roku* period (A. D. 1688–1704).

Those who become skillful can spin the *hakata-goma* upon a slender branch or upon a wire, Fig. 37. The writer says that he does not know when the *bai mawashi* began. Country people take conch shells to play with, and grind the pointed heads flat and the tips round, and wind a cord

---

[1] "Red wood." The *Dictionnaire Coréean-Français* defines it as "Brazil wood."

[2] The city of Hakata, in the province of Chikujen, where it may be supposed this top was first made or came into use.

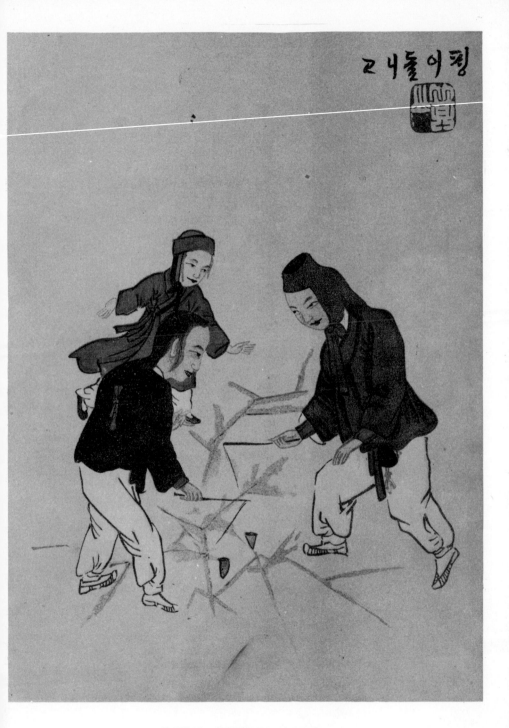

PLATE VI.   KOREAN TOP SPINNING.

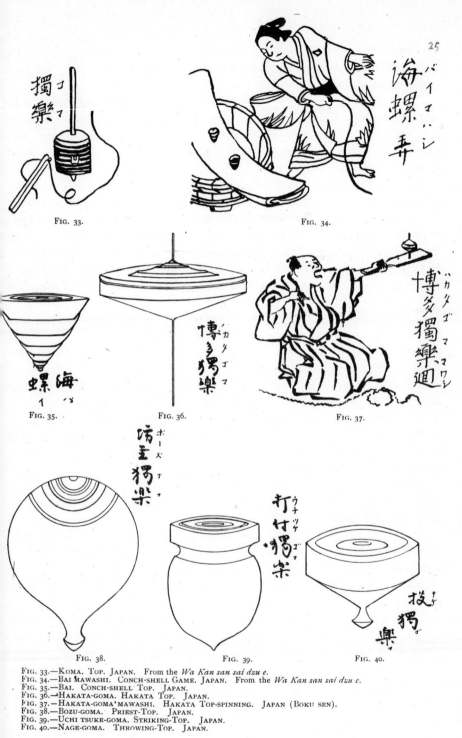

獨樂　ゴマ

海螺弄　バイ　マ　ハ　シ

螺海　ヰ　ハ

博多獨樂　カタ　ゴマ

博多獨樂廻　ハカタ　ゴマ　マワシ

坊主獨樂　ボーズ　ゴマ

打付獨樂　ウチ　ツケ　ゴマ

投獨樂　ナゲ　ゴマ

FIG. 33.

FIG. 34.

FIG. 35.

FIG. 36.

FIG. 37.

FIG. 38.

FIG. 39.

FIG. 40.

FIG. 33.—KOMA. TOP. JAPAN. From the *Wa Kan san sai dzu e.*
FIG. 34.—BAI MAWASHI. CONCH-SHELL GAME. JAPAN. From the *Wa Kan san sai dzu e.*
FIG. 35.—BAI. CONCH-SHELL TOP. JAPAN.
FIG. 36.—HAKATA-GOMA. HAKATA TOP. JAPAN.
FIG. 37.—HAKATA-GOMA'MAWASHI. HAKATA TOP-SPINNING. JAPAN (BOKU SEN).
FIG. 38.—BOZU-GOMA. PRIEST-TOP. JAPAN.
FIG. 39.—UCHI TSUKE-GOMA. STRIKING-TOP. JAPAN.
FIG. 40.—NAGE-GOMA. THROWING-TOP. JAPAN.

around them to spin them with on a mat-tray.[1] Two or three shells are necessary to constitute a game.

The shell that is knocked out of the tray loses. The one that goes in first is called *ika* (Chinese, *i ká*), and the one that goes in last *dai wu* (Chinese, *nai tsz'*). When they collide with each other and go out together, it is called *haru* (Chinese, *chéung*). In this case the *ika* wins. The shells from Kumano[2] are good and strong.

I am informed by Mr. Matsuo that only the tips of the shells are used, and that they are weighted with lead. Good ones cost as much as one to one and a half yen. The game is still very popular at Osaka. Mr. Morimoto has sketched a great variety of tops which are current at the present day in Japan. Among the commonest is the *bozu-goma*, or "priest-top," Fig. 38, which is so called from its resemblance to the shaven head of a Buddhist priest. It is played with a cord, and is usually made of *tsuge*, or box-wood.

A similar top with a sharp iron peg is used by boys in Nagasaki in a top-fighting game like that practiced by American children. The *uchi tsuke-goma*, or "striking-top," Fig. 39, has its upper surface painted with rings of red, and is also played with a cord.

The *nage-goma*, or "throwing-top," Fig. 40, is usually made of box-wood, and is played with a cord, being thrown directly on the ground, or with a sideways motion. The *uke-goma*, or "catching-top," Fig. 41, is made of wood, with an iron spindle around which the cord is wound. This top is thrown sideways, and caught in the hand, or it may be taken up in the hand when spinning on the ground.

The *tsumami-goma*, or "pinching-top," Fig. 42, has an iron spindle, on the upper part of which is a loosely-fitting tube by which the top may be lifted with the fingers.

Little children frequently play with tops, which they twirl with their fingers or between their hands, such as is represented in Fig. 43, under the name of *te-goma*, or "hand-top," or *hineri-goma*, "twirling-top." The spindle is made of bamboo, and the body of wood, with incised rings, which are painted red, on its face.

Fig. 44 represents another form of top which is spun with the fingers, called *kashinomi-goma*, or "acorn-top." The body of the top is made of an acorn, with a bamboo spindle.

---

[1] This consists of a folded mat, as shown in the picture.
[2] A district of Kishiu.

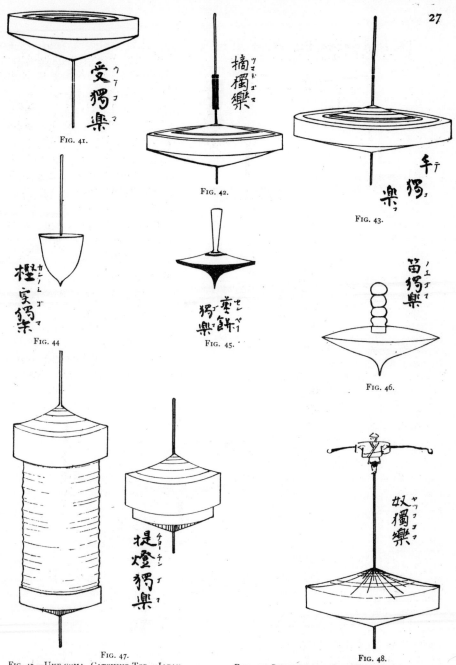

FIG. 41.

FIG. 42.

FIG. 43.

FIG. 44

FIG. 45.

FIG. 46.

FIG. 47.

FIG. 48.

FIG. 41.—Uke-goma. Catching-Top. Japan.
FIG. 42.—Tsumami-goma. Pinching-Top. Japan.
FIG. 43.—Te-goma. Hand-Top. Japan.
FIG. 44.—Kashinomi-goma. Acorn-Top. Japan.

FIG. 45.—Senpei-goma. Cake-Top. Japan.
FIG. 46.—Fur-goma. Whistle-Top. Japan.
FIG. 47.—Chochin-goma. Lantern-Top. Japan.
FIG. 48.—Yakko-goma. Slave-Top. Japan.

The *senpei-goma*, Fig. 45, so called from the cake which it somewhat resembles, is also spun with the fingers.

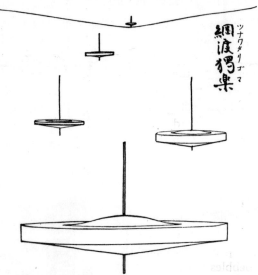

Fanciful tops are common in Japan, such as the *fue-goma*, or "whistle-top," Fig. 46; the *chochin-goma*, or "lantern-top," Fig. 47, made in two parts, connected with paper like a lantern, which distends when it is spun; the *yakko-goma*, or "slave-top," Fig. 48, which has a *mame ning yo*, or "bean-doll" (Fig. 27), at the top; the *tsuna-watari-goma* or "walking the rope top," Fig. 49, and the *komochi-goma*, "child-bearing top,"

FIG. 49.—TSUNA WATARI-GOMA. WALKING THE ROPE TOP. JAPAN.

Fig. 50, which contains a number of small tops, which are released when the top is spun. Many other tops, modifications of these described, are also known.

The top represented under the general name of *koma* in the *Wa Kan san sai dzu e*, Fig. 33, is a humming-top. Humming-tops are known in Japan as *kaminari-goma*, or "thunder-tops." They are made of a section of bamboo, with wooden ends, through which a bamboo spindle is passed.

Fig. 51 represents a Japanese humming-top in the University Museum, which is

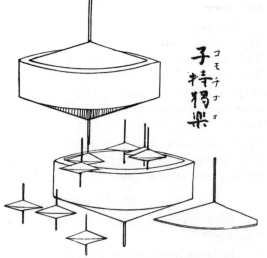

FIG. 50.—KOMOCHI-GOMA. CHILD-BEARING TOP. JAPAN.

rudely painted with flowers. It is identical in form with a bamboo humming-top from Java in the same collection.

XIV. MAI-AM-TOL-KI—SPINNING ROUND.

This game is played by little boys. A boy will draw a circle on the ground, and, crossing his arms, will take hold of one of his ears. He will then stand within the circle and turn around in the same direction until he steps outside of the ring. His companions count the number of turns. He may turn either to the right or left, accordingly as he grasps the right or left ear with his hand.

In Japan little children spin around, holding their ear with their hand, in the same manner as in Korea.

XV. TAK-TCHONG—POP-GUNS.

Boys made various kinds of guns of bamboo. Pop-guns, in which paper wads are used, are called *tji-tak-tchong* (Chinese, *chi*, "paper"—*ch'ung*, "gun"). Blow-guns, in which pebbles are thrown, are called *mo-ri-tak-tchong*. Boys put a needle in a piece of reed and blow it from a hollow bamboo. Squirt-guns for water are also made, called *moul-tak-tchong*.

Japanese boys make pop-guns out of bamboo, which they call *kami-deppo*, or "paper-guns." They also make blow-guns out of bamboo or wood. The latter are preferred, and are usually hexagonal in shape instead of round. A bamboo dart feathered with paper is used in them. These guns are called *fuki ya*, "blow-arrow." They also make bamboo

FIG. 51.—KAMINARI-GOMA,
THUNDER (HUMMING) TOP. JAPAN.
Museum of Arch., Univ. of Penna.
No.

squirt-guns, called *midzudeppo*, "water-guns." In China (Kwangtung) boys make pop-guns of bamboo, which they call *tá pic pok*.[1] They also make squirt-guns out of bamboo, which they call *shui chit*, "water-squirts."

XVI. NA-KOUI—(SQUASH) DONKEYS.

Boys mount a squash, *ho-pak*, on four sticks to make a *na-koui*, "donkey."

In Japan boys imitate animals in the same way with egg plants and radishes. These are made to represent horses or donkeys, and are especi-

---

[1] The last two words are colloquial and mimictic.

ally made at the festival called Bon,[1] that commences on the eve of 13th of the seventh month. The custom was very common in ancient times.

XVII. MOU-TEUNG—TURNIP-LANTERNS.

Boys make lanterns out of turnips in the autumn. These "turnip-lanterns," *mou-teung*, have a window cut in them, which is covered with a piece of paper. Japanese boys make lanterns out of watermelons after eating the pulp.

XVIII. SSI-TEU-KI—WOOF TAKING (CAT'S CRADLE).

Cat's cradle is usually played by girls. The figures which are the same as in our own children's play are named as follows: 1. *Sang-tou-tou-ki*, "cover for hearse;" 2. *Pa-tok-hpan*, "chess-board;" 3. *Tjye-ka-rak*, "chopsticks;" 4. *Soi-noun-kal*, "cow's eyeball;" 5. *Tjyel-kou-kong-i*, "rice-mill pestle."[2]

In Japan cat's cradle is called *aya ito tori*,[3] "woof pattern string-taking." The figures are identical with those in Korea, but receive different names. The first I have been unable to learn; the second is called *nekomata*, defined as "a mountain cat into which a domestic cat is supposed to transform itself;" the third, *koto*, "a musical instrument," or *geta no ha*, the two pieces of wood under the sole of clogs; the fourth, *umano me*, "horse-eye," and the fifth, *tsuzumi*, "a musical instrument."

In Southern China "cat's cradle" is called *kang sok*, which means literally "well rope." It is spoken of as an amusement of girls, but is known to all the Cantonese laborers of whom I have inquired concerning it. They make the same figures as those of Korea and Japan, but do not, they tell me, give them names. The order of the figures, after the first, is not necessarily that here given.

Miss Fielde[4] says that the Chinese (Swatow) call cat's cradle "sawing wood," "in allusion to the final act in the performance."

---

[1] The "feast of lanterns," celebrated at the full moon.

[2] The fingers receive the following names in Korea: Thumb, *mo-tji* (Chinese *mo chi*), "mother finger;" index, *sik tji* (Chinese, *shik chi*), "eating finger;" middle, *tjyang-tji* (Chinese, *ch'êung chi*), "long finger;" third, *mou-myeng-tji* (Chinese, *mo ming chi*), "no name finger," and little finger, *tjă-tji* (Chinese, *tss' chi*), "little" or "son finger." The same names, among others, are given to the fingers in China.

[3] Hepburn's *Dictionary* defines *aya* as "cat's cradle."

[4] *A corner of Cathay.* New York, 1894, p. 87.

XIX. KEM-EUI-TJYOUL-TCHAI—SPIDER WEB (NET) BAT.

A hoop of about one or two feet in diameter is made of a branch of a scrubby tree which the Chinese call *nau*, to which a handle is attached. Boys go out early in the morning and catch spider-webs upon the hoop until it is covered, and later capture locusts, *măi-am-i*, and dragon-flies, *pălk-a-syong-i*, in the net thus formed. When a dragon-fly is captured, it is customary to stick a piece of straw through its abdomen and release it. The insect then mounts directly into the air. This is called " sending into exile."

In Japan, boys use a hoop of bamboo covered with spider-web, which they call *kumono ami*, or " spider-net," to catch locusts, but the same net is also used to catch dragon-flies. They usually catch dragon-flies with *mochi*, or bird-lime, but it is considered more dexterous to seize them with the fingers. It is customary for them to attach a piece of paper to the abdomen of a dragon-fly, and then release it. In going in search of dragon-flies, they generally recite a certain poem. Superstitious people do not catch a certain kind of dragon-fly having a red appearance. The reason given at Tokio is that these dragon-flies make their appearance at the Bon festival; at Nagasaki they say that the spirits of the dead return to earth riding upon their backs at that time.

XX. RYOU-KAIK-TJYO—DELAY GUEST INSTRUMENT (RING PUZZLE).

Ryou-kaik-tjyo (Chinese, *lau kák ch'á*), or " Delay guest instrument," is the name given to the familiar ring and bar puzzle which the Chinese call *kau tsz' lín wán*, or " nine connected rings," Fig. 52. My Korean informant tells me that this puzzle is said to have been invented, according to a Chinese story, by the famous Chinese hero, Hung Ming[1] (A. D. 181–234), who gave it to his wife when he went to the war. The story

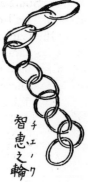

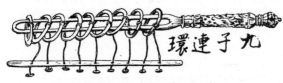

FIG. 52.—KAU TSZ' LIN WÁN. CANTON, CHINA.
Museum of Arch., Univ. of Pennsylvania. No. 7,626.

FIG. 53.—CHIYE NO WA.
RING PUZZLE. JAPAN.

relates that she forgot her sorrow in attempting to solve it. In Japan there are a great variety of ring puzzles, which are known as *chiye no wa*, or " rings of ingenuity." A simple form is represented in Fig. 53. I am

---

[1] *Chinese Readers' Manual*, No. 88.

unable to learn that the first represented ring puzzle is commonly known in Japan.

XXI. MAL-NONG-TJIL-HA-KI—PLAYING HORSE.

Little boys play riding a stick, which they call *mǎl*, "horse." They generally take their grandfather's cane. The same name is applied to riding a stick, and to riding astride another boy's shoulders.

FIG. 54.—TAKE UMA. JAPAN.
From the *Wa Kan san sai dzu e.*

In Japan, little boys play "horse," which they call *take uma*, "bamboo horse." They sometimes have a stick with a horse's head, with bridle and reins, Fig. 54.

The *Wa Kan sai dzu e* relates that T'áu Hien, of the Later Han Dynasty (A. D. 25–221), when fourteen years old, made himself a flag, rode on a "bamboo horse," and played. Kán Kung observed his appearance, and admired it, and granted him his daughter as a wife. His wife indignantly said: "The boy of the T'áu family plays too much. How can we give him our daughter?" Kán Kung replied: "He has a noble aspect, which certainly presages great success," and he gave him his daughter.

The same book states that boys of seven years of age take pleasure in the "bamboo horse."

XXII. NYANG-PAN-NO-RAM—NOBLEMAN PLAY.

A boy bends his back while two boys each take one of his hands and a fourth boy then rides on his back.

A similar game is very popular among Japanese boys. One bends his back and seizes the girdle of another boy who precedes him, while a third rides. The rider is called *Taishō*, or "general," and the game consists in a contest between two riders, who endeavor to pull each other down.

XXIII. HYENG-KA-RAI-TJIL-TCHI-KI.

This is a form of punishment applied as a forfeit in games. The loser is swung by four boys, each one taking an arm or leg until he becomes very tired. The name of this game is derived from the operation of spading practiced by farmers—a kind of shovel shod with iron, *ka-rai*, which is di-

양모는쇽질레가

PLATE VII.   KOREAN SPADE SHOVELLING.

rected by one man, who holds the pole or handle, while two or four men drag the implement by two or four ropes, as shown in Plate VII., is used for the purpose.

XXIV. AING-KEUM-TJIL.—HOPPING.

The one who hops farthest wins.

This is a very common amusement in Japan, where the players usually race to a goal. The name for hopping varies greatly in the different provinces. In Tokio it is called *chin chin mago mago ;* in Aidzu, *biko biko ;* in Shonai, *kata ashi tobi ;* in Yamaguchi, *ken ken tobi ;* in Shimabara (Hizen), *gishi gishi*, and in Kagoshima, *sukkengyo*.

In China (Kwangtung) hopping, called *chik kéuk*, is a favorite amusement with boys.

XXV. TTOUI-EM-TTOUI-KI—JUMPING.

Boys jump standing, and running, from a mark. The running-jump is called *pa-ram-ttoui-em ;* literally, "wind jump." Boys sometimes jump over a rope, and sometimes practice jumping down from high places.

In Japan (Nagasaki) jumping is practiced as an amusement by boys under the name of *tobikko*. A rope is stretched and boys jump over it, or they compete in jumping on the level, sometimes running to obtain impetus.

XXVI. TTOUI-YE-NEM-KI—JUMPING OVER (LEAP FROG).

This game is played by several persons, one of whom leans over, putting his hands on the ground, and the others, who stand behind him, vault over his back by placing their hands upon his shoulders.

Leap frog is a very common game in Japan, under the name of *tobi-koshi*, "jumping over," Fig. 55.

XXVII. TJOUL-NEM-KI—ROPE-JUMPING.

FIG. 55.—TOBI-KOSHI. LEAP FROG. JAPAN.

Jumping rope is a spring game, played only by boys. One turns and jumps by himself. In Japan boys jump rope, one turning and jumping, or sometimes two turn and one or two jump. It is also called *tobi koshi*, or *tsuna tobi*, " rope jumping," Fig. 56. In China (Canton) jumping rope, which is played occasionally by one boy, who turns and jumps, is called *t'iŭ shing*, "jumping rope."

XXVIII. NEL-TTOUI-KI—BOARD-JUMPING (SEE-SAW).

This is practiced especially by girls, even by those of nineteen and twenty years. The two players stand on the end of the board, which is laid on a roll of mats as a fulcrum, and alternately jump up and down. Plate VIII. represents two country girls playing on the *nel-ttoui-em*, or see-saw.

The see-saw is a common game in Japan, where it is called " see-saw," the name having been introduced with the game from Europe or America, Fig. 57. In China (Canton) see-saw is called *tang t'in p'ing*.

FIG. 56.—TOBI KOSHI. JUMPING ROPE. JAPAN.

XXIX. TCHYOU-TCHYEN, OR KEU-NEUI—SWINGING.

Swings are suspended from branches of trees, or where there is no available tree two poles are erected as a support. Young men and women

FIG. 57.—SEE-SAW. JAPAN.

of the same family often swing together. Grown men also practice swinging. The object is to go as high as possible and touch the branches of the tree.

PLATE VIII.　KOREAN SEE-SAW.

Swinging is a spring sport, common in the fifth month. Plate IX. represents two country girls about eighteen years of age, swinging.

In Japan men and boys swing, both the swing and the act of swinging being called *Buranko*, Fig. 58. In China (Kwangtung) swinging is called *Tá ts'au ts'in.*

XXX. TJOUL-TA-RI-KI—ROPE-PULLING (TUG-OF-WAR).

This is played by any number of boys at a certain time of year, about the 15th of the first month. In the country the entire population of districts and villages engage against other districts or villages at this season. It is believed that the village that wins will have a good harvest. The rope is of straw, two feet in diameter, with its ends divided into branches. The men take the main stem, and the women the branches. The latter frequently do more than the men, as it is customary for them to load their skirts with stones on these occasions. The *Dictionnaire Coréen Français* gives the name of this rope as *Kei-tjoul*, and defines it as a " rope which they pull by the two ends to secure abundance."

FIG. 58.—BURANKO. SWING. JAPAN.

The Tug-of-war is a common amusement among school-boys in Japan

FIG. 59.—TSUNA HIKI. TUG-OF-WAR. JAPAN.

under the name of *Tsuna hiki*, or " Rope-pulling," [1] Fig. 59. Another similar

[1] According to *The Japanese Months*, on the 15th day of the eighth month, in the old calendar, people turned out to admire the full moon and made offerings to it of *dango*, a kind of cake made

Japanese game is played by two persons who sit opposite to each other with a cord passing around their necks. They each endeavor to pull the other over. This is called *Kubi hiki*, or "Neck-pulling."

XXXI. SSI-REUM-HA-KI—WRESTLING.

A rope is usually tied around the right thigh to furnish a hold. Shoulder.

is placed to shoulder, and the object is to throw the opponent. In the country grown people wrestle, and a prize is frequently given to the winner. There are no professional wrestlers, as in Japan. Wrestling is commonly known as *Sumo*[1] in Japan, and a wrestler as *sumo tori*, Fig. 60.

The following interesting and suggestive account of wrestling in Japan I have extracted from Mitford's *Tales of Old Japan*.[2]

The first historical record occurs in the sixth year of the Emperor Suinin (B. C. 24), when one Taima no Kéhaya, a noble of great stature and strength, boasting that there was not his match under heaven, begged the Emperor that his

FIG. 60.—SUMAI. WRESTLING. JAPAN.
From the *Wa Kan san sai dzu e.*

strength might be put to the test. The Emperor accordingly caused the challenge to be proclaimed; and one Nomi no Shikuné answered it, and

---

of rice, beans, and sugar. The sport known as "Tug-of-war"—in Japanese *Tsuna-hiki*, or "Rope-pulling"—afforded amusement on the same evening to the boys of rival villages, or to contending parties belonging to the same place, grown-up persons sometimes joining in the fun. Each party furnished itself with a large rope made of rice-straw, having a loop at one end. A stick was passed through the two loops, thus uniting the ropes, and then the two sides commenced to tug. Whichever party was pulled over the dividing line was derided and crowed over, and the same ignominy befel the party whose rope happened to break during the strain. This practice, however, is now a thing of the past.

From the middle of July to the middle of August is an anxious period for the farmers, whose rice plants are in danger of perishing from lack of water, should no rain fall for several consecutive days.

[1] Hepburn's *Japanese English Dictionary* gives the following additional names: *Jidori*, *Yawara* and *Jujutsu*.

[2] *Tales of Old Japan*, by A. B. Mitford, London, 1871. Vol. I, pp. 203–207.

PLATE IX.   KOREAN SWINGING.

having wrestled with Kéhaya, kicked him in the ribs and broke his bones, so that he died. After this Shikuné was promoted to high office, and became further famous in Japanese history as having substituted earthen images for the living men who, before his time, used to be buried with the coffin of the Mikado. In the year 858 A. D., the throne of Japan was wrestled for. The Emperor Buntoku had two sons, called Koréshito and Korétaka, both of whom aspired to the throne. Their claims were decided in a wrestling-match, in which one Yoshirô was the champion of Koréshito, and Natora the champion of Korétaka. Natora having been defeated, Koréshito ascended his father's throne under the style of Seiwa. In the eighth century, when Nara was the capital of Japan, the Emperor Shômu instituted wrestling as part of the ceremonies of the autumn festival of the Five Grains, or Harvest Home; and, as the year proved a fruitful one, the custom was continued as auspicious. The strong men of the various provinces were collected, and one Kiyobayashi was proclaimed the champion of Japan. Many a brave and stout man tried a throw with him, but none could master him. Rules of the ring were now drawn up; and in order to prevent disputes, Kiyobayashi was appointed by the Emperor to be the judge of wrestling-matches, and was presented, as a badge of his office, with a fan upon which were inscribed the words the " Prince of Lions." The wrestlers were divided into wrestlers of the eastern and of the western provinces, Omi being taken as the centre province. The eastern wrestlers wore in their hair the badge of the hollyhock; the western wrestlers took for their sign the gourd-flower. Hence the passage leading up to the wrestling-stage was called the " Flower Path." Forty-eight various falls were fixed upon as fair—twelve throws, twelve lifts, twelve twists, and twelve throws over the back. All other throws not included in these were foul, and it was the duty of the umpire to see that no unlawful tricks were resorted to. It was decided that the covered stage should be composed of sixteen rice-bales in the shape of one large bale, supported by four pillars at the four points of the compass, each pillar being painted a different color, thus, together with certain paper pendants, making up five colors, to symbolize the Five Grains.

The civil wars by which the country was disturbed for a while put a stop to the practice of wrestling; but when peace was restored it was proposed to re-establish the athletic games, and the umpire Kiyobayashi, the " Prince of Lions," was sought for; but he had died or disappeared, and could not be found, and there was no umpire forthcoming. The various provinces were searched for a man who might fill his place, and one Yoshida

Iyétsugu, a Rônin of the province of Echizen, being reported to be well versed in the noble science, was sent for to the capital, and proved to be a pupil of Kiyobayashi. The Emperor, having approved him, ordered that the fan of the " Prince of Lions " should be made over to him, and gave him the title of Bungo no Kami, and commanded that his name in the ring should be Oi-Kazé, the " Driving Wind." Further, as a sign that there should not be two styles of wrestling, a second fan was given to him, bearing the inscription, " A single flavour is a beautiful custom." The right of acting as umpire in wrestling-matches was vested in his family, that the " Driving Wind " might for future generations preside over athletic sports. In ancient days, the prizes for the three champion wrestlers were a bow, a bowstring, and an arrow. These are still brought into the ring, and at the end of the bout the successful competitors go through a variety of antics with them.

To the champion wrestlers—to two or three men only in a generation—the family of the " Driving Wind " awards the privilege of wearing a rope-girdle. In the time of the Shogunate, these champions used to wrestle before the Shogun. At the beginning of the seventeenth century (A. D. 1606) wrestling-matches as forming part of a religious ceremony were discontinued. They are still held, however, at the shrines of Kamo, at Kiyôto, and of Kasuga, in Yamato. They are also held at Kamakura every year, and at the shrines of the patron saints of the various provinces, in imitation of the ancient customs. In the year 1623 one Akashi Shiganosuké obtained leave from the Government to hold public wrestling-matches in the streets of Yedo. In the year 1644 was held the first wrestling-match for the purpose of raising a collection for building a temple. This was done by the priests of Kofukuji, in Yamashiro. In the year 1660 the same expedient was resorted to in Yedo, and the custom of getting up wrestling-matches for the benefit of temple funds holds good to this day.

According to *The Japanese Months*[1], autumn is the season when wrestling is most indulged in throughout the empire of Japan at large, although it is indulged in any period of the year in Tokyo and other large cities. Professional wrestlers are huge fellows, who wear their hair like Spanish bull-fighters, in a style different from that of most other people. They are divided into bands, each under a leader, who gives instruction in the art to his followers, and these companies go from place to place.

---

[1] Vol. II. September.

In Tokyo, wrestling contests generally take place at Ekoin, and continue for ten days at a time. There is a raised arena, encompassed by a
double circle of straw bags filled with earth—sixteen bags in the inner
circle, and twenty in the outer one. Four pillars, which support a roof,
have the lower part hung with red blankets, swathed round with white,
and the upper parts colored respectively Green, Red, White, and Black, to
represent Spring, Summer, Autumn, and Winter. Two tubs of water, salt,
and sheets of paper are provided, and two fans, a bow, and bow-string are
attache᠎ to one of the pillars, to be given as prizes in final contests. After
certain op᠎᠎ing formalities have been performed by the judge, he summons
by name tw᠎ ᠎ombatants from the rival parties, who thereupon advance and
squat upon their heels in the arena. At a signal from the round fan in the
judge's hand, the men rise and grapple with each other, and at the end of
each bout the judge indicates by his fan the side to which the victor belongs.
One use of superannuated wrestlers is to act as umpires, and to compose the
quarrels which sometimes arise among the younger men—quarrels in which
men of ordinary muscle do not care to interfere.

XXXII. HTAIK-KYEN-HA-KI—KICKING (*Fr. Savate*).

Htaik kyen-ha-ki is a combat between two players, chiefly with the
feet. They take their positions with their feet apart, facing each other, and
each endeavors to kick the other's foot from under him. A player may
take one step backward with either foot to a third place. His feet, therefore, always stand in one of three positions. One leads with a kick at one
of his opponent's legs. He moves that leg back and kicks in turn. A high
kick is permitted, and is caught with the hands. The object is to throw the
opponent.

This game also occurs in Japan, but the Chinese laborers from Canton
do not appear to be familiar with it.

XXXIII. TJYE-KI TCHA-KI—SHUTTLECOCK KICKING.

The Korean shuttlecock consists of a flattened ball made of cotton
cloth and filled with clay or ashes, having a feather from a pheasant's tail
stuck in the top. Shopkeepers play the game in the streets to keep their
feet warm. The *Tjye-ki* is kicked from one person to another, and may be
put in place to kick with the hand. The Chinese character *kin*, " foot-ball,"
is given as an equivalent for *Tjye-ki* in the *Dictionnaire Coréen-Français*.
Tcha-ki, " kicking," is apparently from the Chinese *tik*, " to kick."

Plate X. represents country boys kicking the shuttlecock, which the artist has designated as *Myen*.

In Japan the girls only play with the shuttlecock, Fig. 61. It is their customary amusement at the New Year. They use a battledore, *Hago ita*, Fig. 62, usually made of *Kiri* wood, or in the cheaper kinds of *Sugi* or cedar, and having pictures, such as famous actors, on one side. The *Hago*, or shuttlecock, Fig. 63, is made of the seed of the *Mokuran*[1] into which several small feathers are fastened.

FIG. 61.—HAGO ASOBI. SHUTTLECOCK PLAY. JAPAN. (BOKU-SEN.)

The foot-ball seems more nearly allied to the Korean *Tj y e - k i* than the above-described shuttlecock. The *Wa Kan san sai dzu e* gives an account of Foot-ball under the title of *Kemari*, with the Chinese equivalent of *Tz'uk kuk* "Kicked ball," Fig. 64. It quotes the Sán Tz'ai t'ú hwui as saying that the Po Wuh Chí and Liú Hiáng's[2] Pieh luh relate that Foot-ball was made by Hwang Tí.[3]

The *Wa Kan san sai dsu e* also says that some say the Foot-ball originated in the time of the Contending States (A. D. 220–280). It declares

---

[1] The soap-berry tree. Japanese children make soap-bubbles with the skin of this fruit.

According to *The Japanese Months* it was customary before the Restoration to send a stand with two ornamental bows and arrows to houses where there was a male infant, and a battledore and shuttlecock where the baby was a girl among the presents to friends and relations in December. From this it would appear that the battledore had an emblematic significance; probably from its name, that of the woman's paddle used in washing clothes. This seems to be in a measure confirmed by the use of the seed of the soap-berry tree as a shuttlecock, although I have no evidence that the soap-berry was ever used in washing in Japan.

[2] Liú Hiang, B. C. 80–9. One of the most celebrated philosophers and authors of the Han dynasty.—*Chinese Reader's Manual, No. 404.*

[3] The Yellow Emperor, B. C. 2697.

PLATE X. KOREAN KICKED SHUTTLECOCK.

that kicking the Foot-ball is a military resource, the ability of soldiers being tested by play, which furthermore explains military tactics.

FIG. 63.—HAGO. SHUTTLE-COCK. JAPAN. Museum of Arch., Univ. of Penna. No. 16,302.

羽子板
ハゴ
イ
タ

FIG. 62.—HAGO ITA. BATTLEDORE. JAPAN. Museum of Arch., Univ. of Penna. No. 16,301.

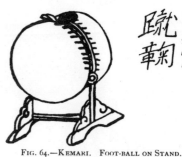

FIG. 64.—KEMARI. FOOT-BALL ON STAND. From the *Wa Kan san sai dzu e.*

The ball is a round bag made of leather and filled with hair, Fig. 63. The Emperor Ch'êng Ti of the Han dynasty took great pleasure in the game.

Japanese annals relate that Foot-ball came to Japan in the time of the Empress Kōgioku;[1] but she, being a woman, did not play it. In the first year of *Tai Ho,* in the time of the Emperor Mommu, Foot-ball was first played. The ex-Emperor Gotoba[2] extolled the game. General Asukai Masatsune was also an

[1] A. D. 642–644.
[2] Reigned A. D. 1184–1198.

excellent player. He made rules for the game, and from this time the foot-ball club began. Among the generals, Minamoto Yoriye played the game very skillfully.

Tradition says that the *Dainagon* Narimitsu was an excellent player. The same work says that one day three strange men came. They had human faces and bodies of monkeys, and resembled children of three or four years. When questioned, they answered they were the spirits of Foot-ball. Each had on their foreheads golden letters : One, *Shun yō kwa* (Chinese, *ch'un yéung fá*), " Spring willow blossom ;" another, *Ka an rin* (Chinese, *há on lam*) "Summer-

FIG. 65.—KEMARI ASOBI. FOOT-BALL PLAY. JAPAN. (BOKU-SEN.)

rest forest ;" and the third *Shū en* (Chinese, *ts'au ün*) " Autumn garden." They said they always lived in the willow forest and were fond of visiting the foot-ball ground. Henceforth we will be its presiding divinities. They then departed. The words, such as *ya kwa*, *an ri*, and *en ū*, which are now cried in the foot-ball place, are the inscriptions on their foreheads. At present they are the gods of ball, which are called *Sei dai myo jin*. They are worshiped on the day of *Midzunoto Saru*, that is, one of the days of the monkey. Their shrine is at the ancient seat of Lord Narimitsu.

According to a note in Mitford's *Tales of Old Japan*,[1] " the game of

---

[1] Vol. I, p. 168.

Foot-ball was in great favor at the Japanese Court. The days on which it took place were carefully noted in the *Daijôkwan Nishi*, or Government Gazette. On the 25th of February, 1869, for instance, we find two entries: 'The Emperor wrote characters of good omen,' and 'The game of Foot-ball was played at the palace.'"

During the days of the extreme poverty of the Mikado and his Court, the Asukai family, notwithstanding their high rank, were wont to eke out their scanty income by giving lessons in the art of Foot-ball.

The picture by Boku-Sen, Fig. 65, represents ancient Japanese nobles of the highest rank playing Foot-ball.

The Chinese laborers in the United States, who come from Kwangtung, are not familiar with hand-ball or any games of ball played with a bat or racquet. They played, however, a kind of shuttlecock with their feet, similar to *Tjye-ki*.

Their shuttlecock, called *Kai mò in*, "Chicken-feather swallow," Fig. 66, consists of several pieces of snake-skin, about

FIG. 66.—KAI MO IN. SHUTTLECOCK.
CANTON, CHINA.
In the author's collection.

one inch and a half in diameter, weighted with a Chinese "cash" or coin, with several feathers stuck in the top. Playing the game is called *T'ek in*, "Kicking the shuttlecock." They are also familiar with a game called *T'ek k'au*, "Kicking balls," which consists in rolling iron balls, about an inch and a half in diameter, with the feet.

XXXIV. MOUL-HTAIK-KYEN-HA-KI—WATER-KICKING.

This is a contest practiced in bathing, the boy who endures longest winning. The Japanese have a similar sport, splashing the water with their hands, which they call *Midzu kake*, "Water-splashing."

XXXV. SYENG-SSA-HOM—DAM-COMBAT.

Two parties of boys each build a dam in a stream. When the upper one is broken, if the lower one endures, that side is regarded as the winner. Japanese children build dams in the same kind of a contest.

XXXVI. TJOU-MEK-TCHI-KI—FIST-STRIKING.

One boy puts down his fist and another endeavors to strike it with his fist. If he hits it he continues to strike, but if the other boy succeeds in drawing away his fist so that the striker's fist hits the ground, the latter loses, and must put his own fist down.

This is played by Japanese boys in the same manner. One player puts down his fist, and the other holding his fist above it cries, *Kokuzo! Kokuzo! Yoi Kokuzo!* As he utters *Yoi Kokuzo*, he brings his fist down, and the other, who must not remove his fist until he hears these words, then draws it away, trying to escape being hit. *Kokuzo* is the name of a Buddha,[1] and the imprecation means, Kokuzo! Kokuzo! Good Kokuzo!

XXXVİI. SYOU-PYEK-TCHI-KI—HAND-CLAPPING.

Two players stand opposite to each other and make certain motions of their hands simultaneously in a given order until one of them misses and loses. Each first strikes his thighs with the palms of both hands, and then, in the same manner, his breasts. Then he claps his hands and strikes his outstretched left hand with the right. Then he claps his hands, and strikes his outstretched right hand with the left. The hands are then clapped, and opened, palms out, to strike those of the other player, and then both clap their hands. The last movements, commencing with clapping the hands, is thrice repeated, when both commence as at first. The motion becomes more and more rapid, and the play becomes very difficult.

This game is played in precisely the same manner in Japan, where it is a common amusement with both children and adults. It is usually played to the accompaniment of songs, and receives the name of *Ken* (Chinese, *k'ün*), "fist." There are several methods of play, which are distinguished by the first words of the songs accompanying them.

The same name, *Ken*, is applied in Japan to a large number of games played by two persons with the hands and fingers. One of the commonest of these games is *Ishi Ken*, or "Stone *ken*," usually called *Janken*. In *Ishi Ken* the fist is called *ishi*, "stone;" the open hand, *kami*, "paper," and the extended index finger and thumb,[2] *hasami*, "scissors." The players extend

---

[1] Chinese, *Hü hung tséung*, identified with *Hü hung chü*, Sanskrit, *Akas'a Pratichthita*, "dwelling in empty space." A fabulous Buddha living somewhere to the south of our universe. Rev. E. J. Eitel, *Hand-book for the Student of Chinese Buddhism*, London, 1870, p. 5.

[2] In the northern part of Japan this is the custom, but in Tokyo the forefinger and middle finger are extended.

their hands simultaneously. Stone beats scissors, as scissors will not cut stone. Paper beats stone, as paper will wrap up stone, and scissors beat paper, as scissors cut paper. *Janken* is often used to decide who shall perform some duty or task. Thus, jinrikisha men play it to determine which is entitled to a passenger. In this case it is customary to cry " one, two, three," which is uttered as a thrice-repeated hissing sound before each decisive movement of the hand.

Mushi Ken, or " Reptile *Ken,*" is played like *Janken.* The thumb is called *hebi,* " snake;" the forefinger, *kairu,* " frog," and the little finger, *namekuji,* " slug." The snake beats the frog, the frog the slug, and the slug the snake.

These may be regarded more as play than as serious games. Such is not always the case with the following game of *Ken,* commonly known as *Kitsune Ken,* or " Fox *Ken.*" In *Kitsune Ken,* the two hands slightly bent forward and raised to the ears is called *kitsune,* " fox;" the two hands placed on the thighs in the respectful posture, *shōya,* " the headman of a village," and the extended forefinger, *teppō,* " gun."

In this game *kitsune* beats *shōya,* because the fox can deceive the man ; the *shōya* beats *teppō,* because the gun may not shoot the magistrate, but the *teppō* beats the *kitsune,* because the gun kills the fox.

There are a great variety of positions in which the hands may be placed to represent the figures in *Kitsune Ken,* no less than twenty-five different attitudes being used for *kitsune,* and ten, it is said, for *shōya.*

Kitsune Ken is said to be more properly called *Tō Hachi Ken,* after an itinerant quack doctor named Tō hachi, some two hundred years ago, when the game was very popular. Instruction is regularly given in *Tō Hachi Ken* by teachers of the game, who are usually schoolmasters. In Tokyo matches are held at places devoted to the game, such as the *Kotobuki Tei.* The announcement is made by circulars and an admission charged. Many hundred spectators assemble, and from 70 to 120 contests are held during the day and evening. A structure, *shi hon bashira,* " four posts," consisting of a square pavilion, supported by four bamboo posts, is erected for the players. This pavilion is similar, only smaller, to that used in wrestling, and the posts are colored in the same manner—green, red, white, and black—to represent the four seasons. The players sit opposite to each other at the sides of the pavilion, within which a small narrow table, *ken dai,* is placed, upon which they rest their elbows. Two umpires, called *Gyoji* and *Mukogyoji,* who have fans, *gumbai,* like those used by umpires in wrestling, sit on the other sides. At the corners are four men called *Toshiyori*, " Elders," who watch the game. They are usually experts who have retired from contests. They are appealed to when a controversy arises. They are called respectively Asakusa, Shiba, Kanda, and Kojimachi, *Toshiyori*, from the four principal wards of Tokyo, which they are supposed to represent. Small prizes are given, such as inexpensive watches or *kimono* (coats) to the successful players.

Another popular game of *Ken* is *Satsuma Ken* (Fig. 67). The players extend the fingers of one or both hands simultaneously, and at the same time endeavor to guess the number put out by the others, crying the

number aloud. They use Chinese words in this game, as follows: *ichi, rian, san, osai, go, roku, chet, tama, kwai,* " one, two, three, four, five, six, seven, eight, nine." This game is the same as the common Chinese game of guessing the fingers, *Ch'ái múi*, and its Chinese origin in Japan is confirmed by its other common Japanese name of *Tōjin Ken,* or " Chinese *Ken*."

FIG. 67.—SATSUMA KEN. JAPAN (BOKU-SEN).

Like the simple hand-clapping games, with which they are sometimes combined, the more complicated games of *Ken* are frequently played as amusements to the accompaniment of songs and music. One of the songs, well known to many tourists in Japan, is as follows:

> *Chonkina, chonkina*
> *Chon, chon, kina, kina,*
> *Chochonga, na no ha de* [1]
> *Chochonga choi!*

At the end of the last line the motion is consummated, the hands keeping time through the song. When a second round is commenced, the verse is varied, the winner singing:

> *Chon kata, chon kata,* [2]
> *Chon, chon, kata, kata*

---

[1] Instead of *na no ha de*, *yoi ya sa de* is substituted.　[2] *Kata*, " won."

and so on, and the loser:

> *Chonmake, chonmake,*[1]
> *Chon, chon, make, make.*

The game of *Ken* is often played in Japan for forfeits (*batsu*, " punishment "). A common one is *sake batsu*. A cup of *sake* is placed between the players, which the loser is required to drink at the end of each round. Sometimes the loser must sing or dance, according to agreement, and when the *gaishas* play for the entertainment of guests they frequently remove their ornaments and apparel until they divest themselves entirely of their clothes.

" Hand-clapping " is played in China (Kwangtung) under the name of *P'ak chéung,* or " Clapping-hand." The game is a common amusement among children. The two players sit opposite to each other. First they clap their hands. Then they clap each other's right hands and clap their hands. Then they clap each other's left hands and clap their hands. These motions are continued alternately, faster and faster, until one makes a miss. Chinese counterparts also exist of the Japanese games, such as *Ishi* and *Kitsune Ken*, as will be seen from the following account given by Miss Adele M. Fielde:

" In many games a servitor or leader is chosen in the following way: The children stand in pairs, and each suddenly thrusts out an arm with one digit extended from the closed fist. One or the other in each pair is vanquished if he holds out a finger reckoned to be of lesser power than the one extended by his neighbor. The thumb is counted as the local idol, the forefinger as a fowl, the middle finger as a gun, the ring-finger as a fox, the little finger as a white ant. If the thumb be opposed to a forefinger the thumb vanquishes, because fowls are commonly slain as offerings to idols. If a thumb be opposed to a middle finger the thumb vanquishes, because a god is greater than the gun, which is often used to announce the presence of the gods. If a thumb be opposed to a ring-finger, there is neither a victory nor a defeat, because gods and foxes are supposed to be always on friendly terms, and so there must be another trial. If a thumb be opposed to a little finger the thumb is vanquished, because white ants often devour idols. If a forefinger be opposed to a middle finger the latter is victor, because guns destroy fowls. If a forefinger be opposed to a ring-finger the former is conquered, because foxes eat fowls. If a fore-

---

[1] *Make,* " lost."

finger be opposed to a little finger the latter is defeated, because fowls eat white ants. If a middle finger be opposed to a ring-finger the latter is defeated, because guns kill foxes.. If a middle finger be opposed to a little finger there must be another trial, because guns and white ants have no mutual influence. If a ring-finger be opposed to a little finger the same result follows, because foxes and white ants have no known relation to each other for either good or ill. When the vanquished in each couple is declared, then these defeated ones pair off and compete among themselves until a servitor is announced by the showing of the last pair of hands.[1]

Hand-clapping is played by children in the Eastern United States in practically the same manner as in Eastern Asia. The game is played with the accompaniment of the following verse, the players clapping their hands as they utter each word :

> " Peas porridge hot,
>   Peas porridge cold,
>   Peas porridge in the pot,
>   Nine days old."

The movements are as follows : (1) clap knees with both hands (*peas*), (2) clap hands (*porridge*), (3) each clap right hands (*hot*), (4) clap knees with both hands (*peas*), (5) clap hands, (6) each clap left hands (*cold*), (7) clap knees with both hands (*peas*), (8) clap hands (*porridge*), (9) clap each other's hands (*in the pot*), (10) clap knees with both hands (*nine*), (11) clap hands (*days*), (12) clap each other's hands (*old*). In Brooklyn, N. Y., this order is reversed, 7, 8, 9, 10, 11, and 12 preceding 1, 2, 3.

In the next movement the players clap their hands, then clap left hands, then clap hands, and then clap each other's hands.

The game is commonly known among children in the United States by the first line of the verse, but I was informed in Montgomery County, Pennsylvania, that it was called " Slap the Quaker," or " Box the Quaker."

The Romans and the ancient Greeks and Egyptians were familiar with the fist and hand-clapping games, of which they appear to have had a great variety. They are figured by Mr. Edward Falkener in his *Games Ancient and Oriental*,[2] from which I have taken the following picture of the hand-clapping game played by two young Egyptian girls, from the tomb of Ak-hor.

---

[1] *A Corner of Cathay*, pp. 80–81.   [2] London, 1892.

XXXVIII. MEK-KOUK.

A boy will take several pine nuts, *tjat*, in one hand and hold out both hands. Another boy then endeavors to point out the hand that contains the nuts. If he succeeds he wins them, but if he fails he pays an equal

Fig. 68.—Hand-Clapping Game. Ancient Egypt. From *Games Ancient and Oriental.**

number. Another way is for several boys to each take pine nuts in one hand, and cross the fingers holding the nuts. Then each guesses the total number, and the one who guesses correctly takes all.

The *Dictionnaire Coréen-Français* defines *Mek-kouk* as follows: *Nom d'un jeu de hasard qui consiste à deviner combien d'objets sont cachés dans la main d'une personne* (*Si on tombe juste, on gagne un jeton*), and gives the Chinese word *k'ün*, " fist " (see No. xxxvii) as an equivalent.

The Japanese play a similar game which they regard as a kind of *Ken*, but which receives the name of *Nanko*,[1] or " What number ?"

---

* With the kind permission of Messrs. Longmans, Green & Co., New York.

[1] Hepburn's *Dictionary* gives *ts'ong kau* " hiding hook " as the Chinese equivalent for *nanko*.

Two persons play, using three small pieces of wood, which usually consist of pieces of chop-sticks, about half an inch long. One takes the sticks and holds them out to the other on the outstretched palm of his left hand. He then clasps his closed right hand upon the left hand containing the sticks and cries *san !* "three!" This is repeated and then he holds out his right hand closed, inviting the other to guess. The latter makes signs with his fingers or cries out a number, "one," "two," or "three." If he fails to guess, the other shows him the sticks, and repeats the operation; but if he guesses correctly, he is given the sticks, and his opponent guesses. The player who first loses three times must drink a cup of *sake*, whereupon the game begins over again.

A game similar to *Mek-kouk* is played in China (Kwangtung) by boys. One boy will take some small object, a stone or a nut, in his hand and cover it with his other hand and swing both hands clasped over the object up and down, repeating the following lines :

> *Luk kú luk tung kwá*
> *Pau kwo pau kwo t'ong*
> *Ts'ü shéng, ts'ü há ?*

At the last line he will draw his fingers apart, and the other will guess whether the object is above or below. At the close of the last line he holds his hands apart, one above and one below, and the other player guesses in which hand the object is concealed.

XXXIX. SONG-TJANG-TCHAT-KI—CORPSE SEARCHING.

One boy is blinded, and the others hide a stone or some small object under a mat or in a hole in the ground. The one who is it asks, " Did you bury it?" The reply is, " Yes," and he then endeavors to find it.

In Japan a popular game is called *Kakushi ko*, "Thing hiding."

XL. KO-NO-TTEU-KI.

This game was not known to my informants.

The *Dictionnaire Coréen-Français* defines it as a game which consists in the players sticking a little stick in the sand in which a ring has been concealed. The one whose stick passes through the ring wins.

XLI. MOUT-KO-TCHAT-KI—HIDE AND FIND.

Another game of concealing a stone is played as follows : Three or four engage. One boy takes a stone in his hand, and, making a fold in another boy's coat, places the hand holding the stone in the fold, and, on withdrawing it, the owner of the coat holds up the fold as though it contained the stone. This is repeated with one or more players, and finally the first boy holds out his closed fist. Another boy now guesses where the stone is concealed, whether in one of the boys' coats or in the first p ayer's fist, and if he guesses correctly he takes the stone and hides it.

XLII. NEUNG-KYEN-NAN-SA.

A boy will hide a slip of paper between his fingers and alternately raise and set down two cloth cuffs. The other players then guess under which cuff the slip of paper is concealed.

The name *neung-kyen-nan-sa* (Chinese, *nang kin nan sz'*) means something that is seen without being understood. The *Dictionnaire Coréen-Français* says that thus is called the twelve vases of the same size that fit one into another in any order in which they are placed.

XLIII. SYOUM-PAK-KKOUM-TJIL-HA-KI—HIDE AND SEEK.

One boy is blinded while the others hide. A boy who remains with the one who is " It " beats his back when all have concealed themselves.

The game is played in the same manner in Japan under the name of *Kakurembo*—" Hiding."

XLIV. SYOUN-RA-TJAP-KI—WATCHMAN CATCHING (TAG).

One boy is called the *Syoun-ra* (Chinese, *ts'un lo*), or watchman, and chases the others, endeavoring to catch them. The one who is caught becomes the *Syoun-ra*. When a boy sits down and says " *taik-kok*," he may not be caught. The one who shall be *Syoun-ra* at first is decided by drawing straws.

According to law and custom in Korea, men are not allowed to go out at night, this privilege being accorded to women alone. When a man meets a woman in a public place he must turn away his head, thereby intimating that he does not see her. An explanation of these customs is to be found in the fact that, according to primitive belief, man belongs to the masculine principle of the universe, the sun, and therefore to the day, while woman belongs to the feminine principle, the moon, and therefore to night. The *Syoun-ra* is the night watchman, whose duty it is to enforce the custom prescribed by this mythic ordinance.

In Japan, the one who is " It " in tag is called *Oni*, " Devil," and the game is called *Oni gokko*, or " Devil playing." The game is frequently played

4

with stations, called *hashira*, "posts,"[1] at which the players may take refuge.

XLV. SYOUN-RA-PAP—DRAWING STRAWS.

The boy who gets the longest straw becomes *Syoun-ra*. The name *syoun-ra-pap*, applied to drawing straws, means literally "watchman repast," and was explained to me by the statement that the watchman is supposed to get a good supper for his night's services.

Drawing straws is practiced in Japan by boys, who call them *kujï*, "lots."

As many straws are used as there are players, and the one who gets the longest or the shortest straw, as may be agreed upon, becomes the *Oni*.

Drawing straws is practiced in China (Canton) by boys under the name of *Ts'im ts'ò*. A boy will hold two straws of unequal length in his hand and invite another to draw one of them. If the drawer gets the longer straw, the holder pays him one "cash," but if he gets the shorter straw, he pays the holder one cash. Boys in Canton frequently decide which shall perform an appointed task by drawing straws, the one getting the shorter losing. Six boys sometimes play the following game:

Six straws are tied in two sets of three each. Each boy chooses a projecting end, and the threes who get the same sets become partners. The two sides draw again for position. The losers seat themselves on three stools placed to form a triangle and put their feet together. The others then endeavor to jump in from the three sides. Another similar game, called *T'iù lung mín*,[2] or "Jumping the dragon's gate," is played by four boys, as follows: The players pair off by one of them holding two straws by the middle. Each boy seizes a projecting end, and those who get the same straw become partners. One will now offer a long and a short straw to one of his opponents to draw for position. If he draws the short straw, the drawer loses, and *vice versa*. The loser and his partner seat themselves on two stools, facing each other, and, leaning their bodies backward, raise and spread their legs apart, with the soles of their feet pressed each against the other's. The boys who are out now stand on either side and, one at a time, endeavor to jump into the space between the seated players' legs. As one runs, the other endeavors to distract the attention of the seated ones, and there feints, with the efforts made to keep the players from jumping in,

---

[1] Referring to the posts or pillars of the house.
[2] This expression is also used metaphorically for "rising rapidly in (literary) degrees" (Williams's *Tonic Dictionary*).

and with their falls and other misadventures furnish the amusement of the game.

The custom of drawing straws appears to be closely associated in China, if it did not indeed originate, in ceremonial divinations with straws and splints.

XLVI. COUNTING OUT.

It is also customary for boys to determine who shall be *Syoun-ra* by counting out, for which purpose the following rhyme is used. It is the only one my informant ever heard:

Ha-nal-tăi,
Tou-al-tăi,
Sam-a-tjyoung,
Na-al-tăi,
Ryouk-nang,
Ke-tji,
Hpal-tăi,
Tjang-koun,
Ko-tou-răi,
Pping.

It may be translated in part as follows:

" One time,"
" Two times,"
" Three *a tjyoung*,"
" Four times,"
" Six *nang*,"
" *Ke-tji*,"
" Eight times,"
" *Tjang-koun*,"
" Nine *tou-răi*,"
" *Pping*."

Counting-out rhymes are also used in Japan to determine who shall be *Oni* in games. The following was related to me from Shonai, where boys use it to determine the guilty one when an offense has been committed, as well as in games:

Hi fu no da
Da Daruma da no da

Chin kuruma
Chin no chin.[1]

The following line is also occasionally repeated around in counting out: *Fuku toku bin*, "happiness, virtue, poverty." This is more frequently used, however, in a kind of childish fortune-telling, to decide the future of the individuals of the company.

Chinese boys use a variety of counting-out rhymes. The following was related to me by a boy from Hoh Shán, Kwangtung:

> *Tim tim tsz' nip*
> *Shui t'ò shui mat nip*
> *Shéung shui yam*
> *Há shui nip*
> *Kam chí fú yung*
> *Má tsz' héung shai*
> *Páu pák pò*
> *Pák páu pò á tsai*
> *Á tsai mí tò loi*
> *P'ai yan om ngán*
> *P'ai yan nip*
> *Chuk tò fán loi*
> *Tsau k'ü tsít.*

They employ this rhyme in determining who shall be "It" in hide and seek. The boy who is "It" is called *Ping*, "soldier," and those who hide *Ts'ák*, "thieves." Counting out is commonly spoken of as playing *Tim tim tsz' nip*.

XLVII. KA-MEK-TJAP-KI—IN THE DARK CATCHING (BLIND-MAN'S BUFF).

When the one who is "It" has his or her eyes blinded, the game "Blind-man's Buff" is called *Ka-mek-tjap-ki*, "In the dark catching." It is played in the house for fear of injury to the players. The one who is "It" is called *Syoun-ra* as in the preceding, and in games of "Tag" generally. Plate XI represents boys, and Plate XII, girls, playing Blind-man's Buff. It is designated by the artist as *Noun-ssa-mái-ki*, or "Eye hiding."

In Japan the game of Blind-man's Buff is called *Me kakushi*, "Eye hiding." It is customary for the players to clap their hands and cry:

---

[1] *Hi fu*, "one, two;" *no* means "of;" Daruma is the idol (cf. No. 1), and *kuruma* means "wagon."

눈싸미기호ㄹ

PLATE XI.　KOREAN BOYS PLAYING BLIND MAN'S BUFF.

> *Yura san! Yura san!*
> *Te no naru hō, ni?*
> " Yura san! Yura san!"
> " Hands sounding direction, I say ?"

This is taken from a popular play about the " Forty-seven Ronins." In one of the scenes the hero, Yura San, enters a brothel, where he plays Blind-man's Buff with the girls, who cry to him as above.

Miss Fielde[1] gives the following account of Blind-man's Buff at Swatow, China :

" Blind-man's Buff is played under the title of ' Fishing-by-hand.' A limit is set, beyond which none may pass during the game. The leader holds her right arm level, with the palm of her hand downward, and the other players touch her palm with the point of the index finger. Whoever she can catch, by suddenly closing her hand upon the finger, must put on the blinder and become ' fisherman.' If the blinded fisher call out, saying, ' the tide is rising,' the fish must clap their hands to suggest their activity in high water ; but if the fisher says, ' the tide is falling,' then the fish must steal about cautiously, as if they had but little water to sport in. When a fish is caught, the fisher must guess its name before taking off the blinder."

XLVIII. HKOU-TO-RONG-KOING.

Two boys start from same place and run in opposite directions around a square. When they meet on the opposite side they stop and play a game of *Ko-no* (LXXVI). Usually before the game is finished one pushes the other over. They then resume their race around and the one who arrives first becomes the winner. Sometimes, instead of playing *Ko-no*, they exchange objects they hold in their hands. The name of the game is said to be an imitation of the sound of the band of drums and cymbals at the head of a military procession.

XLIX. O-RANG-HKAI-KKOT-TCHI-KI—VIOLET FIGHTING.

Country children gather violets, *o-rang-hkai-kkot*, or " barbarian flowers," and fight them by striking the stalks so as to break the heads off. This is played by Japanese children under the name of *Hana sumō*, " flower wrestling." Morrison's *Dictionary*,[2] under the character *Tuy*, gives the following account of a similar Chinese game :

---

[1] *A Corner of Cathay*, p. 82, 83.   [2] Vol. I, p. 516. Macao, 1815.

" ' The whole party of children, having plucked flowers and grass, came and squatted themselves down in the midst of the pile of flowers and grass to fight grasses.' Each child doubles the grass or stem of the flowers, and taking the two ends in his fingers, forms a hook which is linked to the grass of his opponent, hooked in the same manner. They both pull, and the child whose grass breaks first loses; sometimes it is mere play, at other times they stake a cash, about one-fourth of a half-penny, on each chance. This early gambling is discountenanced by correct parents."

L. HPOUL-TCHI-KI—GRASS GAMING.

When country boys go out to cut forage for the cows they are often more inclined to play than work. Each boy will gather a bundle of grasses and flowers, and all will sit down to play. One will lay out a piece of grass or a flower, which the others must match. If they cannot match it it is laid to one side and is counted against them.

When boys are cutting grass, one will hold the sickle and let it fall. If the point sticks he wins, and the other boy must pay a small bundle of grass, but if it fails to stick he must pay. This receives the same name as the preceding. Japanese boys play with the sickle in the same manner.

LI. YET-TCHI-KI—CANDY GAMING.

Two boys will each buy a stick of candy [1] and break it in half. The one whose stick has the biggest hole in the middle wins, and the other must pay for both.

LII. AING-TO-CHI-KI—CHERRY GAMING.

Aing-to-tchi-ki (Chinese, *ying t'ò*, " cherry ") is played in the season of cherries, when two boys engage. One will wager another that he cannot take say forty cherries in his mouth, and separate the stones from the pulp without swallowing a single stone. The other boys who may be present eat what they want, and then, if the boy swallows a single stone, he pays for all, but if he succeeds the one who wagered pays.

LIII. NEUNG-KEUM-TCHI-KI—APPLE GAMING.

Two boys play. Each cuts an apple, or two apples, in half. They divide and count the seeds in their portions, and the one who has the highest number wins.

---

[1] Made of rice, and corresponding with the Japanese *ame*, which is sometimes made in the form of sticks.

양ㅗ눈ㅎ기미사눈

PLATE XII.   KOREAN GIRLS PLAYING BLIND MAN'S BUFF.

LIV. KOM-TCHI-KI—PERSIMMON GAMING.

This is played like "Apple gaming" (No. LIII).

Guessing the number of seeds in a persimmon is a very common game in Japan among the lower classes, under the name of *Kaki kiri*, "persimmon cutting." One will say five and another six, and so on, and the one who guesses correctly wins the stakes. In Kwangtung, China, guessing the number of seeds in an orange is a common game. This is called *T'au kom piú*, or *Hoi kom piú*, "Opening orange lottery."

Any number play, and the one who guesses nearest wins. This game is played by men, and not by children.

LV. SAL-KOU-TCHI-KI—APRICOT GAMING.

One boy strikes several ripe apricots with his fist, the number being agreed upon. If all the stones fly out he wins, but if one misses he must pay for all the apricots that have been eaten.

LVI. TCHAM-OI-TCHI-KI—MELON GAMING.

Korean melons are usually very long. One holds the melon and strikes it with the edge of his hand, and endeavors to cut it in half. If he wins the other pays.

LVII. TJYO-KAI-SSA-HOM—CLAM-SHELL COMBAT.

Each boy lets a clam-shell fall two or three feet to determine who shall play first. This is done by the one whose shell falls concave side down. Another boy lays down a shell, and the first player throws a shell at it. If he breaks his opponent's shell the latter must put down another, and so on ; but if he fails he loses his turn.

LVIII. KONG-TCHI-KI—BALL BATTING.

Kong-tchi-ki, or "ball batting," is a game of ball played by larger boys. Two lines or bases are drawn on the ground a number of feet apart, with a dividing line midway between. A wooden ball, *kong*, is placed on the dividing line, and the players, who are divided into two sides, endeavor to knock the ball with wooden clubs across their opponents' base line.

I am informed that a similar game is played at present in Kagoshima, where the Korean potters were settled, and nowhere else in Japan. The

FIG. 69.—KIU JO. BALL STICK (AND BALL). JAPAN.

From the *Wa Kan san sai dzu e.*

game is played with a wooden ball about three inches in diameter, called *hama*, the game being called *Hama nage*, or "*Hama* throwing." It is usually played in the first month. Four persons usually engage on a side, each having a club about three feet long. The ball is placed in the middle between two base lines, and the object is to drive it across the opponents' line. The players stand in a row, and if the first one fails to stop the ball, and the second or third stops it, he takes the place of the first player. When the ball is driven across a boundary, the sides change places. The game is now prohibited by the local authorities on account of its danger.

Ball batting is referred to in the *Wa Kan san sai dzu e* under the name of *Mari uchi* (Chinese, *tá k'au*), "hitting the ball;" where the stick is spoken of *kiu jo* (Chinese, *k'au chéung*), "ball stick." It further says that investigation of the origin of the game of *Mari uchi* shows that it is very remote, both in Japan and China. In recent times it was only played by small boys. Each first month it was played in association with *Hama yumi* (Chinese, *p'o mo kung*), defined by Hepburn as "a bow for driving evil spirits away; also a small bow used by children." "In late years *Mari uchi* has fallen into disuse, and the original form is seldom seen." This account may furnish an explanation of the term *hama*, applied to the ball used in Kagoshima, *hama* meaning in the compound *hama yumi*, "expelling demon."

LIX. HTAING-TJA-TE-TJI-KI—ORANGE THROWING.

Games of throwing ball do not appear to be common in Korea. Children occasionally play with a kind of wild orange called *htaing-tjă*,[1] which grows on the Island of *Tjye-tjyou* (Quelpart). They toss it in the air and use it to pitch and catch. Boys sometimes endeavor to juggle with this fruit, and keep two or more in the air at the same time.

LX. KONG-KEUI—JACKSTONES.

Jackstones are played by boys. Five or seven stones or pieces of brick are used. The game is played upon the ground. There are a great variety of methods. In one, five stones are used. Four are placed upon the ground and one is tossed into the air. Before it falls another is picked up and the one first thrown, which must be caught as it descends, is then put down. The second stone is then tossed and the third picked up, and so on. This is called *al-nat-ki*, "laying the eggs." The four stones are then placed upon the ground beside the left hand, which is held palm down. The fifth

---

[1] The *Dictionnaire Coréen-Français* defines this as *petite orange sauvage*.

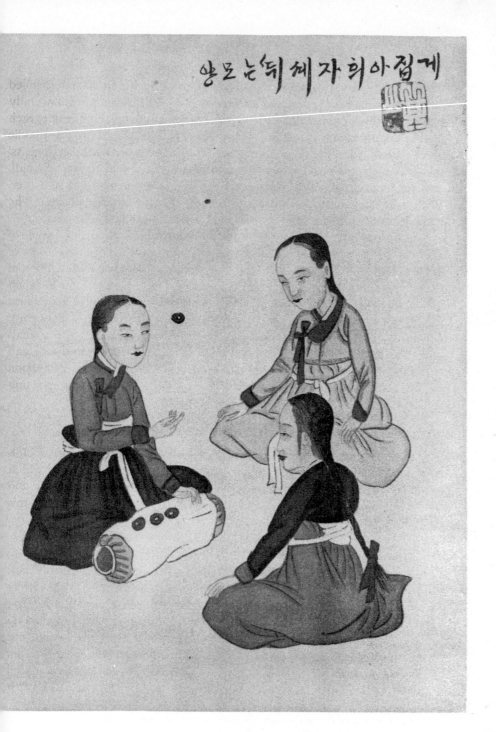

양모눈뒤세자희아접게

PLATE XIII.   KOREAN GIRLS PLAYING TJA-SSEI.

stone is then tossed up with the right hand, and before it falls one of the other stones is struck under the left hand. This, called *al-hpoum-ki*, "setting the eggs," is repeated until all the stones are struck under the left hand, or the player misses. It is followed by the player laying down three stones and holding one in the hollow of his little finger. The fifth stone is then thrown up, and before it falls he must strike one of the stones on the ground with the other in his hand. This is repeated until he strikes all of the three stones in this manner, or misses. The last operation is called *al-kka-ki*, "hatching the eggs."

Girls play a game similar to jackstones with "cash" or coins. Plate XIII represents country girls playing such a game, the name of which is given as *Tja-ssei*.

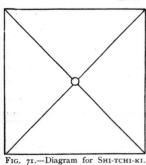

FIG. 70.—ISHI NAGO. STONE THROWING (JACKSTONES). JAPAN.

From the *Wa Kan san sai dzu e.*

The *Wa Kan san sai dzu e* gives the following account of the method of playing jackstones, under the name of *Ishi nago*, or *Ishi nage* (Chinese, *chák shik*), "throwing stones:" A girl takes ten or more stones and spreads them out. She throws one into the air, and before it comes down grasps two or three and catches the one she has thrown. This is repeated, and when she picks up all she wins.

The Chinese laborers in the United States tell me that in Kwangtung jackstones are regarded as a game for little girls. The game is called *Chap tsz'*, "picking up stones."

LXI. SHI-TCHI-KI—METAL STRIKING.

A diagram about two feet square with diagonal intersecting lines extending from the corners is drawn upon the ground. One player puts a small piece of metal where the lines cross in the centre. Another player then endeavors to knock it out of the diagram by throwing at it a round piece of metal about the size of a dollar. If he succeeds the first boy must put down another piece of metal, but if he fails he must put down a piece, and the other throws.

FIG. 71.—Diagram for SHI-TCHI-KI. METAL STRIKING. KOREA.

In Japan a diagram, as represented in Fig. 72, is used in a game of throwing cash. The object is to knock the money out, it being placed in the centre. Each player puts in one *rin*, and they throw in turn.

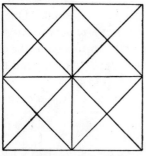

LXII. TON-TCHI-KI—CASH STRIKING (PITCHING PENNIES).

The games of tossing cash are very numerous in Korea, and are among the commonest amusements. My informant believed there were at least ten different ways of playing, of which he described the following :

FIG. 72.—DIAGRAM USED IN GAME OF THROWING CASH. JAPAN.

LXIII. MO-TO-MEK-KI—EATING ALL.

Mo-to-mek-ki is played with ordinary cash or coins, and a heavy piece called *mok-tji*, made by binding five cash together with wire, and filling the hole in the middle with lead. A little hole, about an inch in diameter, is dug, and a line called *oin-son*, or " left hand,"[1] drawn at the distance of a foot from the hole. The first player is determined by each throwing a cash at the hole, and the one who comes nearest plays first and the others in order. If several cash fall in the hole, the one whose cash is on top becomes the first player. The first player stands at a certain distance, and throws all the cash, including his own and those of the others, at the hole. Those that go in the hole he wins. If any go outside of the hole, the other players indicate to him one of them which he must strike with the heavy piece, they selecting the most difficult. If he strikes it he takes all the cash, but if he misses it the second player throws the *mok-tji*, and so on. If the players indicate a piece without the line and nearer the thrower as the one to be struck, he must hold the heavy piece on the fingers of his open hand, and thus throw it.

LXIV. PPYEM-NAI-KI—MEASURE TAKING.

A piece of straw or stick is cut about three inches in length, with which to measure. Two persons play together. One throws four cash at the hole, and the other player must pay as many cash as go in the hole. The latter then points out one of the cash, if any, that went outside of the hole for the

---

[1] The space without this line is called *oin-son*, and that within it, next the hole, *pareun-son* or right hand. It is sometimes required that the player shall strike a piece that falls without the line by throwing the *mok-tji* with the left hand, which may explain the name given to the line.

thrower to strike. If he hits it he wins, and is paid two cash; if he comes within the straw's length he loses his turn, but if outside of this distance he pays two cash.

Many games of tossing cash are played by Chinese children. One of these played in the vicinity of Canton is entitled *Kwang sám man* (*kwang* is a mimetic word for noise; *sám*=three; *man*=coins). In this game the obverse of the cash with the dynastic title is called *pák*, "white," and the reverse *hak*, "black." [1] "White" loses, "black" wins.

Kwang sám man is played by three persons, who each throw a cash on a flat stone for position. If all three coins fall with the same face up, the players throw again. If one falls reverse (black) up the thrower becomes first player, and the others throw for second and third place. If two fall reverse up, the throwers throw again for first and second place. The order decided, the first player takes the three cash in one hand and throws them on the stone. He wins those that fall reverse up, and hands the others, if any, to the second player, and the same continues until all the cash have been won.

FIG. 73.—ZENI UCHI, MONEY STRIKING. JAPAN.
From the *Wa Kan san sai dzu e.*

This game is also called *Kwang ú* [2] *pák*, or *T'iú ú* [2] *pák*, "Playing black and white."

Tiú sám kok, "Pitching at the triangle," is another game played with cash. A man will arrange three cash in a triangle on the ground, and invite children to throw cash at them from a distance of ten or twelve feet. If a thrower's piece falls within a certain distance (about three inches), measured with a small rod, he receives back his own and one cash in addition; if it strikes one of the coins in the triangle he receives back his own and three in addition; but if his piece fails to come within the length of the rod he loses it.

Luk ngau (*luk*="rolling," *ngau*?) is played by two or more children,

---

[1] The writer offers in explanation of these terms the former use of blocks of wood, white on one side and black on the other, such as were anciently used in games in China, and are still current in Korea in the game of *Nyout-nol-ki*, No. LXX.

[2] *Ú*, a "crow," is here used metaphorically for "black."

who each let a cash roll down a smooth stone. The player whose coin rolls farthest from the stone stands toeing the place where it fell, and throws it at the piece nearest his own. If he strikes it he wins that piece, and, toeing it, throws again at the next piece. When he misses the player whose piece rolled next farther up toes the place where his piece fell, and throws at the next one.

LXV. HPAL-MAI-TCHI-KI—STONE-THROWING.

Two or three boys throw and the one throws farthest wins. The loser pays a forfeit, such as treating all to fruit or enduring a punishment as *Hyeng-ka-rai-tjïl-tchi-ki* (No. XXIII).

LXVI. PYEN-SSA-HOM—SIDE OR FACTION FIGHTS.

When a free-born Korean boy reaches the age of fifteen, he has a small wooden label cut, which he carries with him. This label, called *hō-hpai* (Chinese, *hò p'ái*), " name tablet," is made of pear wood or mahogany, and is about two inches in length by one-half inch broad. It is inscribed in Chinese characters. Across the top is the name of the *Pou* (Chinese, *pù*), or ward, to which the boy belongs. Then in a line below, the designation *han-ryang*, " leisure fellow," that is, not in service, and the boy's name with the date of his birth. The date on which the label is made is cut on the reverse. This label must be sealed by an official of the Treasury, who brands it with a hot iron and registers the boy's name and other particulars. When a boy enters the *Tjïn-să*[1] (Chinese, *tsun sz'*), he has another tablet cut, this time of boxwood, with his proper title instead of *han-ryang*. Upon passing the military or civil examinations, the label is cut from black horn, and, upon obtaining the first grade, an ivory label is permitted. The free-born boys jealously guard their right to carry the *hō-hpai*.

The city of Seoul is divided into five *Pou :* the Middle, Eastern, Western, Southern, and Northern. It will, therefore, be seen that all persons are officially enrolled under one of these directions. A knowledge of these facts is necessary for a more correct understanding of the curious contests that take place every winter in Korea, immediately after kite-flying time, that is, after the fifteenth of the first month. These contests, called *Pyen-ssa-hom*, or " Side " or " Faction Fights," are commenced by little boys, who make ropes of straw, *sak-ki*, and fight with them. Sides are formed which retreat and advance. Bigger boys take part, and at last men join in the

---

[1] The second grade of literary rank.

conflict. Stones are the principal weapons employed, with the result that many are killed and injured. We see in this the city boys divided into gangs or bands, and engaging in fights much like the stone fights that used to be common among boys in our American cities.[1]

Japanese boys engage in fights with stones and with snow-balls. These contests, and similar fights, are called *Gempei* (compounded of Gen and Hei), from the names of the famous rival families, Genji and Heiké, Minamoto and Taira. One side represent the Genji and take their colors, white; and the other, the Heiké, and take their colors, red. The rival families were in the East and West, and the sides in these sports may be regarded as associated with these directions, the Genji, East, and the Heiké, West.

When the circumstances of the game demand a division into three sides, it is spoken of as playing *San Goku*, or "Three States," from the old Chinese history of the three contending States of Wei, Wu, and Shu.

"In the first month of the year in the southern provinces of China," according to Archdeacon Gray,[2] "the peasants of neighboring villages meet in the open plains, form sides and attack each other with stones. These encounters are sometimes very serious affairs. . . . They are occasionally attended with loss of life, and the elders of the villages frequently do their best to prevent them."

LXVII. HPYEN-SA-HA-KI.

Archery is practiced as a game at the present day in Korea under the name of *Hpyen-sa-ha-ki* (Chinese, *pin shé*), or "Side shooting." It is usually a contest between different villages or different quarters of the city. The players practice from day to day, and choose the most skillful. Twelve men take part on each side, and there are usually three or four sides. When four parties contest, they each have a different flag. The men on each of the four sides dress alike, and wear similar arm-ties, *hpal-ttji* (Chinese, *pi chi*). The names of the players on the four sides are written on four pieces of paper, on which the scores are kept. The target, *koan yek* (Chinese, *tik*=bull's-eye), is a square board, with a black square in the centre. Each player shoots fifteen arrows in three turns, five at a time. A shot in the centre of the target counts two, and without the centre, one. When a successful shot is made, the shooters on that side wave their flag.

---

[1] Dr. Franz Boas informs me that among the Eskimo there is a custom somewhat similar to that of Korea, the boys born in summer fighting those born in winter.

[2] *China*, London, 1878. Vol. I, p. 256.

Sometimes four singing girls, *kī-săing*, one for each of the four different sides, accompany the shooters, and when a hit is made the girl for that side sings, calling out the name of the person making the shot. The music at the same time strikes up. When the game is closed at night, the music is turned to the place of the victor, whom the other contestants follow, the losers paying for the feast. The winning side takes precedence in the next contest. It is customary for the most skillful shooter on a side to shoot last. The leader of a side is called *hpyen-tjyang* (Chinese, *pín ch'éung*) or *syou-tyeui* (Chinese, *shau tái*), literally, "head belt." The second in order is called *pou-hpyen-tjyang* (Chinese, *fú pin ch'éung*), or *pou-tyeui* (Chinese, *fú tái*), literally, "second belt." The third is called *sam-hpyen-tjyang* or *sam-tyeui* (Chinese, *sám tái*), literally, "third belt;" and the last is called *tjyong-tyeui* (Chinese, *chung tái*), literally, "end belt."

The arrow shooters form a class by themselves, and are united in societies, which, although not as great as at one time, still flourish. They are known as *Han-ryang* (Chinese, *hán léung*), "leisure," or "unoccupied fellows," not in service, being neither nobles nor soldiers. They do no work, but travel from place to place, and are said to think and talk of nothing but arrow-shooting from morning until night. They have their leaders, who are usually two or three old men.

The *Han-ryang* have different organizations in different quarters of the city of Seoul. The Eastern society is called the *Ha-nam-tchon-han-ryang* (Chinese, *há nám ts'ün hán léung*), or Lower Southern village *han-ryang*. This peculiarity is said to be due to the configuration of the city. The Western society is called *Sye-tchon-han-ryang* (Chinese, *sai ts'ün hán léung*), or Western village *Han-ryang;* the Southern, *Năm-tchon-hán-ryang* (Chinese, *nám ts'ün hán léung*), or Southern village *Han-ryang*, and the Northern, *Pouk-tchon-han-ryang* (Chinese, *pák ts'ün hán léung*), or Northern village *Han-ryang*. The flag of the Eastern society is green; of the Western, white; of the Southern, red; and the Northern, azure. The Northern society is generally recruited from the noble boys, and the Southern from the sons of military families. The most distinguished among the *Han-ryang* is the son of a concubine of one of the nobles, called *Koan-han-ryang* (Chinese, *kwán hán léung*). Debarred by his birth from entering civil or military life, he joins the *Han-ryang*. A *Han-ryang* from the country is called in Seoul, *Pyel-pou-nyo*.

The *Han-ryang* retain old customs and traditions. They form a fraternal union, helping each other in trouble, and go about always carrying their bow and arrows, indifferent to public opinion, and doing whatever they

PLATE XIV.   KOREAN BOW MAKER AND HAN-RYANG.

please. During the past four years His Majesty, the King, has suppressed the *Han-ryang*, subjecting them to severe penalties, and it is said that in a few years they will entirely disappear.

Plate XIV represents a *Han-ryang* and a bow-maker, *koung-tjang-i*, who is repairing a bow.

LXVIII. TTJAK-PAK-KI—SINGLE-STICKING (SHOE SHOOTING).

This is a game played by boys with steel-pointed arrows. A mark is put in the ground at a certain distance and those who engage shoot at it. The one who goes farthest away must put his shoe in the place where his arrow strikes, and then all shoot at the shoe, including its owner, until one misses, when he must put his shoe down instead. This game is very destructive to boys' shoes. Shoes are very commonly used as targets by boys in archery in Japan, the shoe being suspended by a cord.

LXIX. PANG-HTONG-I—PITCH POT.

This is described in the *Dictionnaire Coréen-Français* as a game which consists in throwing, with the hand, small arrows into a vase.

My informants tell me that it is not a common game in Korea, but is practiced ceremonially by the *ki-săing*.

The game of Pitch Pot is one of the oldest games of which we have any recorded history. It is described in the Li Ki[1] under the name of *T'au ú*, or " Pitch Pot." From this account it appears that *T'au ú* was a contest at pitching darts into the mouth of a vase placed at a short distance from the players. Two might play at it or any number. The host and guest in the text are representations of two parties or sides. The game is described as being played with much ceremony. The host carries the arrows in both his hands put together; the superintendent of the archery carries in the same way the stand upon which the tallies are placed; and an attendant holds in his hands the pot. The players kneel on a mat two and one-half

FIG. 74.—TSUBO UCHI. PITCH POT.
JAPAN.
From the *Wa Kan san sai dzu e.*

---

[1] Book XXXVII. *The Sacred Books of China. The Texts of Confucianism.* Translated by James Legge, Part III, Oxford, 1885.

arrow lengths from the pot. The tallies or counters vary in number according to the place where the game is played; five, seven or nine sets being used. Each round is with four arrows. The players pitch alternately, and when an arrow enters, the superintendent of the archery kneels and puts down an arrow. When he first asks the players to pitch, he takes up eight counters, whence it would appear that two men were matched at a time, as if they were successful in their four throws, eight counts would be scored. The victor gives the vanquished a cup to drink, and when the cups of decision have been despatched, the superintendent begins to set up what he calls a "horse" for the victor. If he sets up one horse, then a second, and finally a third, he begs to congratulate the thrower upon the number of his horses. From this it seems likely that the winner continues playing against a fresh opponent, the text speaking of the partners of the guest and of the host, who are on the left and right. "Each horse stands for so many tallies."

LXX. NYOUT-NOL-KI—NYOUT PLAYING.

The most popular game in Korea at the present day is known as *Nyout-nol-ki* or "*Nyout* playing." It is played upon a diagram drawn upon a piece of paper or upon the ground, by two, three, or four persons, who move objects used as men around the diagram according to throws made with four blocks of wood used as dice.

The diagram, called *nyout-hpan* or "*nyout* board," consists of twenty-nine round marks, twenty of which are arranged at equal distances in a circle, with an interior cross of nine marks, as shown in Fig. 75. Those at the four quarters and in the centre are larger than the others. The circle at the top is always marked with the Chinese character *ch'ut* (called in Korean *nal-tchyoul*), "to go out." The blocks ordinarily used, called *pam nyout* or "chestnut *nyout*," Fig. 76, are about an inch in length, white and flat on one side and black and convex on the other. They are usually made of the wood of a thick, bushy tree like the prunus, which is used in China for bows, called *Ssa-ri* (Chinese, *nau*), whence the game is called *Sa-ri-nyout*. Another wood, *Pak-tal-na-mou*, defined as a very hard wood, of which mallets are made, is sometimes used for the blocks, but the former is preferred.

The convex side of the blocks is blackened by charring. The fall of a piece with the convex side up is spoken of as *ep-hpc-tjyet-ta*, and with the flat side up as *tjap-pa-tjyet-ta*. They are frequently allowed to fall through a ring of straw about two inches in diameter, affixed to the end of a stick

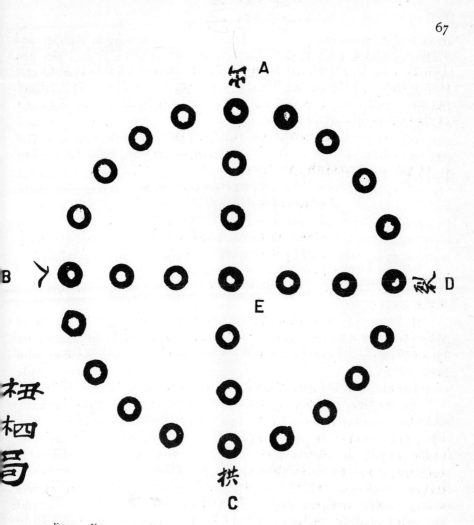

FIG. 75.—NYOUT-HPAN. KOREA. Museum of Archæology, Univ. of Penna. No. 18.569.

FIG. 76.—PAM-NYOUT. KOREA. Museum of Archæology, Univ. of Penna.
No. 16,897.

about a foot long, which is stuck in the ground in the centre of the ring. This is done to render the result of the throws more a matter of chance than of skill. In the picture, Plate XV, the boys are represented as throwing the *nyout* blocks through a cuff, *hto-syou* (Chinese, *t'ó shau*), which one of them has removed for the purpose.

The pieces or men, called *mal* (Chinese, *má*), "horses," may consist of any convenient stick or stone or piece of paper, and are moved according to the throws, which count as follows:

> 4 white sides up, called *nyout*, 4.
> 4 black sides up, called *mo*, 5.
> 3 white sides up, called *kel*, 3.
> 2 white sides up, called *kai*, 2.
> 1 white side up, called *to*, 1.

When a block falls in an upright position it counts as though it fell with the black side up. The players frequently utter loud cries when they throw *nyout* or *mo*.

A throw of *nyout* or *mo* entitles the player to another throw, which he makes before moving his piece. The one who shall play first is determined by throwing the blocks, the highest leading, and the others in the order of their throws.

The players enter their men on the mark next on the left of that marked with the character *ch'ut*, and move around from left to right against the sun, according to their throws. The object of the game is to get from one to four horses, as may be agreed, around the circle and out at A, in advance of the men of the other players. A throw of one more than enough to carry a man to that point is necessary to take it out, but if there is an excess, it does not matter. When two play, each strive to get one or four men around, as may be agreed upon. When three play, each play three horses, and when four play, the winning side must get four horses around. In the latter case those that sit opposite play as partners. If a player throws so that one of his men falls upon another of his own, he may double up the two pieces, and thereafter take them round as one piece, but they count as two in the game. This play is called *kou-et-ta* (Chinese, *ch'an*). The process may be repeated once or twice, depending upon the number of men required to make the circuit. A single "horse" is spoken of as *han-pen-kou-et-ta* (Chinese, *yat fán ch'an*), but when the piece is doubled it becomes *tou-pen-kou-et-ta* (Chinese, *i fán ch'an*); when it is trebled it becomes *sei-pen-kou-et-ta* (Chinese, *sám fán ch'an*), and when three horses have been added it becomes *nei-pen-kou-et-ta* (Chinese, *sz' fán ch'an*). When

아희놋듸긔로르

PLATE XV.   KOREAN NYOUT PLAYING.

a player moves so that his piece falls upon a piece occupied by one of his opponents, the latter's piece is "caught," *tjap-et-ta* (Chinese, *ná*), and must be started again as at first. When a player captures an opponent's piece, it gives him another throw. When a player throws *nyout* or *mo*, and another throw, whatever it may be, he may divide the throws between two pieces. A player may move his partner's pieces. In opening the game a throw of *mo*, or five, takes the player to the spot marked B, and he returns toward the goal by the radius BE. If, on the contrary, the player throws less than five, and his next throw or throws do not terminate upon the mark B, he must continue around the circle, until, if he falls upon the mark C, he may return by the way of CE, EA. If he overthrows the mark C, he must continue on to D, and thence around to A, the going-out place. As ordinarily played upon the ground, the Chinese character *ch'ut* is drawn at the going-out place. Other Chinese characters are sometimes written in the large circles at the sides and bottom. At the left the character *yap* (Korean, *toul-ip*), "to enter;" below, *kung* (Korean, *kot-tjil-kong*), "to arch," or "encircle;" and on the right *lit* (Korean, *tji-tjil-yel*), "to cut through."

When a player first puts a horse on, it is said to be *pout-tchyet-ta* (Chinese, *po*), "applied," and, accordingly, as it enters upon the first, second, third, fourth, or fifth mark, it is spoken of as *to*, *kăi*, *kel*, *nyout*, or *mo-pout-tchyet-ta*. When a horse stops on the first double circle marked with the Chinese character *yap*, it is said to be *en-tjyet-ta* (Chinese, *yap*), "entered." When it stops at the centre, it is said to be *ne-et-ta* (Chinese, *chung yéung*), "centered." When it stops at the bottom, it is said to be *ko-tjyet-ta* (Chinese, *kung*), "encircled;" at the right, *tjeu-tjyet-ta* (Chinese, *lit*), "cut through," and at the top, "tied." When a horse stops on the mark next to the one at the top, it is spoken of as "nearly tied." On going out at the top, it is spoken of as "gone out."

Games with one, two, three, and four "horses," are respectively called *tan-tong-nai-ki* (Chinese, *tán p'at*), "single horse going out;" *tou-tong-nai-ki* (Chinese, *i p'at*), "two horse going out;" *syek-tong-nai-ki* (Chinese, *sám p'at*), "three horse going out;" and *nek-tong-nai-ki* (Chinese, *sz' p'at*), "four horse going out."

In the more classical forms of the game, Fig. 77, Chinese characters, forming an ode, are written within the circles, exclusive of a centre, at which is inscribed the name *Hang Ou*. This form of the game is said to have been written by a scholar of Southern Korea. According to the tradition of the game, the twenty-eight marks represent the horse-soldiers of the famous Chinese general, Hiang Yú,[1] with the general himself in the centre. It is related that when Hiang Yú was defeated by the Prince of Han, he was left alone with twenty-eight soldiers, surrounded by whom he made his successful escape.

The Chinese ode written upon the board refers to an episode in the conflict between Hiang Yú and the Prince of Han, and from the direction in which it must be read would seem to indicate that the original goal in the game was the centre instead of the place at the top. The inscription is as follows : *Hon t'ái tsò sin yap Kwán Chung. Chau Man Wong shui kung P'ing Chéung. Fán tséung kwan tsun lit muk ts'z'. Ch'o pá wong nám ch'ut fúi wai.*

I am informed that the name Hiang Yú is usually written in the centre, but the scholarly Korean who wrote the board or chart represented by Fig. 77, substituted in its place the characters *Chiú-Sin (Tyo-syen)* or Chosen, the present name of the Kingdom of Korea.

Nyout is played for money in the cities by the lower classes, especially in public houses. Parents do not allow their children to play it, and the blocks are confiscated by them and by teachers whenever they are found. Korean boys concealed them in their pockets when these contrivances were imitated from foreigners, but now this is known, and an examination of boys' pockets is made by teachers.

While short blocks, *pam-nyout*, are used by children, and gamblers in cities, in the country, long blocks, called *tjyang-tjak-nyout* (Chinese, *chéung chéuk sz'*) or "long-cut *nyout*" are employed. These blocks, Fig. 78, are usually about eight inches in length. In throwing them, one is often placed across the others which are held lengthwise in the hand by the thumb, with the ends resting on the fingers. This is the conventional way, but not obligatory. When played indoors, they are often made to rebound by striking against the roof of the house. The game is very generally played in this manner by all classes in the country, but only from the 15th of the

---

[1] Hiang Tsi, or Hiang Yú (Koreans write Hang Ou), D. B. C. 201. Nephew of Hiang Liang, and noted from his youth by his great stature and martial prowess. On the downfall of the house of Ts'in, proclaimed himself ruler of the western provinces of Ts'u (corresponding to the modern provinces of Ho-nan and northern Ngan-hwei), whence he is known as Sz' Ts'u Pa-Wang. In B. C. 206, the armies of Ts'in, to the number of 200,000, surrendered themselves to him, and he is said to have butchered them to the last man. He also put to death Tsze Ying, the rightful successor to the throne. In B. C. 205, he similarly murdered the puppet sovereign, I Ti, but upon this his powerful ally, the self-styled Prince of Han, declared war against him, and after a long and sanguinary struggle effected his complete overthrow. When all was lost, he committed suicide at Kai Hia (in modern Ngan-hwei).—*Chinese Reader's Manual,* No. 165.

FIG. 77.—NYOUT-HPAN. KOREA. Museum of Archæology, Univ. of Penna. No. 16,487.

FIG. 78.—TJYANG-TJAK-NYOUT. KOREA. Museum of Archæology, Univ. of Penna. No. 16,898.

twelfth month to the 15th of first month, the season at which visits are exchanged.

The names applied to the throws in *Nyout*, with the exception of the name of the game itself,[1] which is confounded with *ryouk*, "six" (the Chinese character *luk*, "six," being given as its equivalent), are not given in the *Dictionnaire Coréen Français*, nor do they appear to be used in Korea except in connection with this game. Dr. Daniel G. Brinton, who has kindly compared them, tells me that the first three have rather close analogies with the Ural-Altaic stock. The "four" and perhaps the "five" seem connected with the Samoyed.

	Korean.	Ural-Altaic.
1.	*To* or *ta.*	*it, té* (Finnish, Lappish).
2.	*Kăi* or *ká.*	*kaħ* (Finnish, Lappish).
3.	*Kel* or *kol.*	*kol* (Finnish, Lappish).
4.	*Nyout.*	*tet* (Samoyed).
5.	*Mo.*	*sumula* (Samoyed).

It is clearly apparent that these terms are numerals, and they point very directly to the source of the game. A game similar to *Nyout*, played with staves, is recorded to have existed in China in the third century of our era. It was then regarded as a foreign and non-Chinese game, which agrees with the linguistic evidence furnished by the terms used in *Nyout*.

It is customary in Korea to use the long blocks at the 15th of the first month for the purpose of divination. Early in this month a small book is sold in the markets of Seoul to be used in connection with the blocks. The players throw the sticks three times, noting the number that is counted for the throw at each fall. The series of three numbers is then referred to

---

[1] The name of the game, *nyout*, is written in Korea with an obsolete Chinese character which the Koreans read as *să*, having the sound of *sz'* in China. It is formed by compounding the Chinese radical *muk*, "wood," with the character *sz'*, "four," placed to the right, the compound apparently referring in this connection to the four blocks of wood which are used in the game. M. de Guignes in his dictionary gives the sound of the character as *ssí*, with the following definition: *Sorte de spatule dont on se sert pour ouvrir la bouche d'un mort, afin d'y introduire des perles ou autres objets precieux.*

Morrison's *Dictionary* (Macao, 1822) gives the pronunciation as szé, and the meaning, " a sort of spoon;" Keŏ (*kok*) szé, "certain utensils of the spoon kind, used in funeral ceremonies."

Kanghi's dictionary gives two pronunciations for this character: one as the correct pronunciation, like sih, a "breath," and the other as sz, "four;" and the meaning, *pî*, a spoon. "In ceremonial usage it stands for a spoon used to eat the juice of a certain fruit from a cup. Again it is used at the funeral ceremonies." It quotes the Li sáng tá kí chú, or *Book of Funeral Ceremonies*, as saying that the *sz'* must be cut six inches in length and have both ends curved.

the book, upon the several pages of which are printed in Chinese characters all the various permutations of the numbers, taken three at a time, with Korean text explanatory of their significance.

A reproduction of the first page of the section, entitled *Tjyek-să-tjyem* (Chinese, *chák sz' chím*), "Throwing *Nyout* Divination," from a little Korean hand-book, *Tjik-syeng-pep* (Chinese, *chik sing fát*), "Correct Planet Rule," is given in Fig. 79. The numbers represented by the throws are from " one " to " four " in 64 permutations, from which, it will be seen, that only three staves are used. *Nyout*, or " four," is the highest throw, and an explanation is thus given of the name of the game, which is that of the highest throw in the divinatory system from which the game originated.

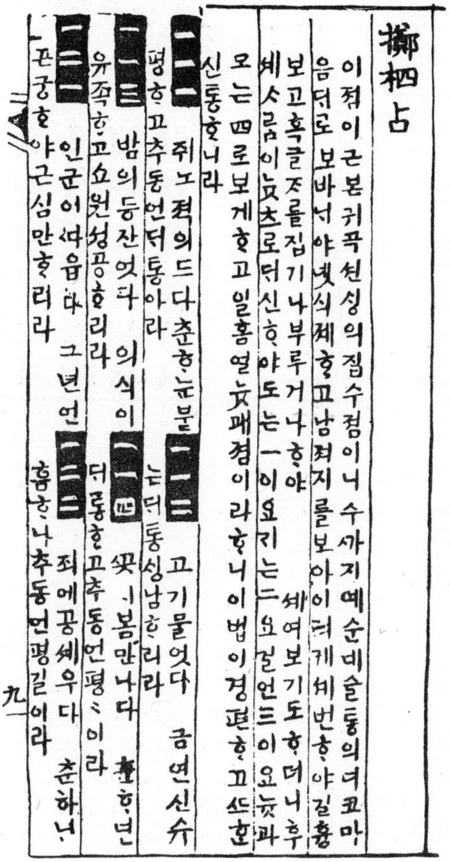

The Chinese *Book of Divination* consists of 64 diagrams, *Kwá*, composed of combinations of unbroken ———— with broken lines ———— ————, six being taken at a time, and the resulting diagrams being known as the Sixty-four *Kwá*, Fig. 80. Each of these 64 hexagrams is designated by a name and is accompanied by a short explanatory text. Now the Sixty-four Hexagrams are regarded as an expansion of the Eight Trigrams, Fig. 81, called the *Pát Kwá*, or " Eight *Kwá*," formed by combining the same unbroken and broken lines three at a time.[1] The unbroken lines in the dia-

Fig. 79.—First page of Tjyek-sa-tjyem.
Korean hand-book for divination with staves.

---

[1] These combinations of triple lines are believed to have been invented by Fuh-hi, the legendary founder of the Chinese polity, as successor to the divine beings who are reputed to have reigned during countless ages before human society was constituted. To further his efforts, it was

grams are called *yéung*, " masculine," and the broken lines, *yam*, " feminine."
It is apparent that if the two sides of the Korean blocks be regarded as

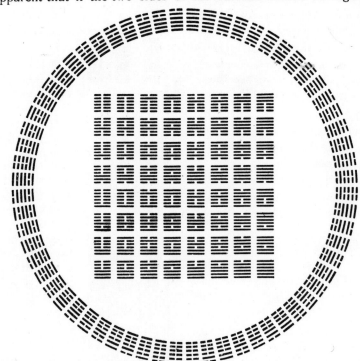

FIG. 80.—THE 64 HEXAGRAMS. CHINA.

representing the unbroken, or masculine, lines and the broken, or feminine,
lines, the trigrams will form a record of the throws when three blocks are

so ordered by Heaven that a supernatural being called the dragon-horse rose from the waters of
the Yellow River and presented to his gaze a scroll upon its back, inscribed with mystic diagrams.
From these and from the movements of the heavenly bodies he deciphered the system of written
characters with which he superseded the method of keeping records by means of knotted cords.

According to the Chinese belief, the eight figures, together with sixty-four combinations to
which they are extended, accompanied by certain presumptive explanations attributed to Fuh hi,
were the basis of an ancient system of philosophy and divination during the centuries preceding
the era of Wên Wang (twelfth century, B. C.), but of which no records have been preserved beyond
the traditional names of its schools or divisions. Wên Wang, while undergoing imprisonment at
the hands of the tyrant Shau, devoted himself to the study of the diagrams, and appended to each
a short explanatory text. . These explanations, entitled *T'un*, with certain further observations on
the strokes of the figures, termed *Tséung*, which are attributed to Chau Kung, the son of Wên
Wang, constitute the work known as Chow-Yih; or, *Book of Changes of the Chow Dynasty*, which,
with the commentary added by Confucius, form the Yih King, the most venerated of the Chinese
classics.—*Chinese Reader's Manual*, Pt. II, No. 241.

used, and the hexagrams when six blocks are taken. This I believe to have been their original purpose. I regard the diagrams as records of possible throws with two-faced staves, and the text that accompanies the hexagrams in the *Yih King*, to be explanatory, in somewhat the same way as the text of the Korean *Tjyek-sã-tjyem* shown in Fig. 79.

FIG. 81.—THE PÁT KWÁ OR EIGHT TRIGRAMS. CHINA.

The Korean game of *Nyout* may be regarded as the antetype of a large number of games which exist throughout the world. Thus the diagram of the Hindu game known as *Pachisi*, or *Chausar*,[1] as illustrated by a specimen in the Museum of the University of Pennsylvania, Fig. 82,

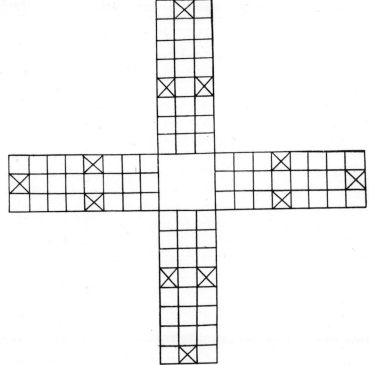

FIG. 82.—DIAGRAM OF PACHISI-CLOTH. MALDIVE ISLANDS. Museum of Archæology, Univ. of Penna. No. 16,476.

will be seen to be an expansion of the *Nyout* circuit with its internal cross. The four large circles at the extremity of the internal cross are represented

---

[1] Called *Pachisi* when played with cowries, and *Chausar* when three long dice are used.

by the *kot*, or "castles," marked with crossed lines upon the *pachisi* diagram, and the count remains the same; the five squares from the end of the arm representing the five circles of the arc and the three squares the radius of the *nyout* circuit.

The chess-board is the square of the arm of the *pachisi* cross. This furnishes a likely explanation of the *koung*, or "palace," of the Korean (Chinese) chess-board, Fig. 93, which appears to be a survival of the *kot*, or castles of the *pachisi* cloth.

In the *Pachisi* game we find the four *mal*, or horses, of the *Nyout* game replaced by four objects of wood or ivory, distinguished by their color, for each player. They are painted with the colors symbolic of the four directions: red, green, yellow, and black. These men, called in Hindustani *goten* (plural of *got*), are doubled in the ancient Hindu game of *Chaturanga*, or dice-chess, each player having eight men, four of which remain unchanged, and four, distinguished by their forms, designated as King, Elephant, Horse, and Ship.

The moves in *Chaturanga* are made according to throws of an oblong four-sided die, similar to the dice used at the present day in India in the game of *Chausar*. This die was marked on its four sides with the numbers 2, 3, 4, and 5. "If on throwing the die the number should turn up 5, the King or one of his Pawns must move; if 4, the Elephant; if three, the Horse, or, if the throw be 2, the Ship must move." Professor Duncan Forbes [1] has clearly pointed out the relations of the four-handed game of *Chaturanga* to our own game of chess. In the former game "it was of the utmost importance with each of the players to get possession of his ally's throne, a step which thenceforth secured to him the individual command of the allied forces. It must, therefore, have often happened that, after some twenty or thirty moves, the contest remained to be decided between two players only." In the two-handed game, one of the allied Kings becomes a subordinate piece, called by the Persians and Arabs *Farzin* or *Wazir*, the queen of our European game.

In addition, the game of *Nyout* may be regarded as the ancestor, or a type of the ancestral form, of the various games played with dice upon boards. These will be referred to under *Tjyou-să-ă*, "Dice" (No. LXXII), and *Ssang-ryouk*, "Backgammon" (No. LXXIII). It has been shown that our game of chess, in which the die has been abandoned, appears to have been derived from it. In the same manner, it appears to have given birth to

---

[1] *The History of Chess*, London, 1860.

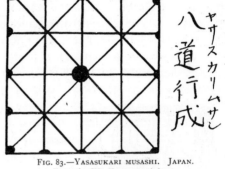

a variety of other board games, of which " Fox and Geese " is a type. This is
well illustrated in the Japanese game of " Fox and Geese," figured in the *Wa
Kan san sai dzu e* under the name of *Yasasukari musashi* (Fig. 83), and commonly known as *Juroku musashi*,
or " Sixteen Soldiers." In this game
we have sixteen soldiers, *Juroku
musashi*, surrounding the general,
Taishō, in the same manner as, according to the tradition, the 28
horse-soldiers surrounded t h e i r
general, Hang Ou.

LXXI. TJYONG-KYENG-TO—THE GAME
OF DIGNITARIES.[1]

FIG. 83.—YASASUKARI MUSASHI. JAPAN.
From the *Wa Kan san sai dzu e.*

This is the Chinese game of the
" Promotion of Officials," *Shing kún
t'ó*,[2] a common game in China and frequently played by the Chinese laborers
in the United States. It is played in Korea upon a printed chart called
Tjyong-kyeng-to-hpan, bearing the name of Korean officials. The moves
are not made according to the throws with dice, as in the Chinese game,
but with respect to the way in which a block of wood turns, which is rolled
from the hand. This block, Fig. 84, called *tjyong-kyeng-to*, is about four
inches long and has five sides, which slope from the middle to the pen-
tagonal ends. Its longitudinal
edges are notched with from one
to five nicks, painted red, and the
moves are made, from one to
five, as one of these numbers
comes uppermost. The various
positions upon the board, which
are inscribed with the names of
the officials of the kingdom, ad-
vance from the lowest to the highest, as in the Chinese game, up to the
title of *Ryeng-eui-tjyeng* (Chinese, *ling i ching*), the first of the three
Ministers of State, or to *Pong-tjyo-ha* (Chinese, *fung ch'iú ho*), explained

FIG. 84.—TJYONG-KYENG-TO.
Museum of Archæology, Univ. of Penna. No. 16,899.

---

[1] *Tjyong-kyeng-to* (Chinese, *sung héung t'ó*) is given as the name of this game in the *Dictionnaire Coréen-Français.* My Korean informant tells me that *Seung-kjeng-to* (Chinese, *shing héung
t'ó*) is the more correct name.

[2] *Chinese Games with Dice.* By Stewart Culin: Philadelphia, 1889, p. 18.

as "retired minister." There is also a third goal called *Htoi* (Chinese, *t'úi*), "retirement."

Tjyong-kyeng-to is permitted in schools, and my informant suggests that the use of the peculiar die is due to the fact that ordinary dice are forbidden to children. However this may be, I am inclined to regard it as a survival, and derived from the staves originally used in the similar game of *Nyout*, with which the game was doubtless originally played.

Plate XVI represents an old man and a young man playing the game.

A die similar to the Korean *Tjyong-kyeng-to* is described as having been used in England, in Easther's *Almondbury Glossary*, quoted by Mrs. Gomme,[1] under the name of Lang Larence:

FIG. 85.—LONG LAWRENCE. ALMOND-BURY, ENGLAND.

Specimen reproduced from description given by Mrs. Gomme. Museum of Archæology, Univ. of Penna. No. 18,257.

"That is Long Lawrence, an instrument marked with signs, a sort of teetotum. A 'Long Lawrence' (Fig. 85) is about three inches long, something like a short ruler with eight sides; occasionally they have but four. On one side are ten x's or crosses forming a kind of lattice-work; on the next, to the left, three double cuts or strokes, passing straight across in the direction of the breadth; on the third, a zigzag of three strokes one way, and two or three the other, forming a W, with an additional stroke or a triple V; on the fourth, three single bars, one at each end and one in the middle, as in No. 2, where they are doubled; then the four devices are repeated in the same order. The game, formerly popular at Christmas, can be played by any number of persons. Each has a bank of pins or other small matters. A pool is formed; then in turn each rolls the 'Long Lawrence.' If No. 1 comes up the player cries 'Flush,' and takes the pool; if No. 2, he puts down two pins; if No. 3, he says 'Lave all,' and neither takes nor gives; if No. 4, he picks up one. The sides are considered to bear the names, 'Flush,' 'Put down two,' 'Lave all,' 'Sam, up one.' It has been suggested that the name 'Lawrence' may have arisen from the marks scored on the instrument, not unlike the bars of a gridiron, on which the saint perished."

LXXII. TJOU-SA-A—DICE.

The Koreans call dice *Tjyou-să-ă*, which appears to be compounded of the Chinese *chü shá*, "vermillion," with the particle *ă*. Their dice are iden-

---

[1] *The Traditional Games of England, Ireland, and Scotland,* by Alice Bertha Gomme. London, 1894. Vol. I, p. 326.

양모 눈치 도졍종

PLATE XVI.   KOREAN GAME OF DIGNITARIES.

tical with those of China, Fig. 86, being bone or ivory cubes, regularly marked on their six sides with spots from one to six arranged so that the sum of any two on opposite sides is equal to seven. The "ones" and "fours" are painted red and the "fours" are larger and more deeply incised than the other spots. Their principal game with dice is *Ssang-ryouk* or Backgammon. The other games with dice known to my informants were one in which

FIG. 86.—CHINESE DICE.

a die is substituted for the four staves in the game of *Nyout* (No. LXX), and another which I am told has no special name, but might be called *Tjyou-să-ă-nol-ki*. Three or four boys sit around and one puts a peanut or pinenut on the floor. Each throws a die, and the one who gets highest wins the nuts. In Japan dice are called *sai*, and in China *shiǐ tsai.*[1]

It may be observed that the Korean game of *Nyout* when played with dice is much the same as the game widely played throughout Europe under the name of the "Game of Goose." [2]

FIG. 87.—JAPANESE CHILDREN PLAYING SUGOROKU.

A similar game is extremely common in Japan under the name of *Sugoroku*, or "Double Sixes," Fig. 87 This name is distinctively that of the backgammon game played with two dice, but it is applied in Japan to all games played upon a board or diagram according to the throws with dice, or a spinning die, *coma* (teetotum). *Sugoroku* is a common amusement of Japanese children at the New Year, when new games are usually published.

LXXIII. SSANG-RYOUK—DOUBLE SIXES (BACKGAMMON).

The game of backgammon is known in Korea under the name of *Ssang-ryouk* (Chinese, *shéung luk*), "Double Sixes." It is played with

---

[1] Medhurst's *English and Chinese Dictionary*, Shanghai, 1847, gives the following additional names for dice : *t'au tsz'*, *luk ch'ik*, and *shéung luk*, the latter, "double sixes," being the name of the highest throw in the game with two dice

[2] Known in France as the *Jeu de l'oie ;* in Italy as the *Giuoco dell oca*, and again in Mexico as the *Juego de la oca*. In northern Europe it is frequently called the "Snake game," as in England, and again in Sweden, where it is known as the *Orm spel*.

wooden pins or men called *mal* (Chinese, *má*), "horses," upon a hollowed wooden board called the *Ssang-ryouk-hpan*. The board has mortised sides, which extend above the surface. The divisions on either side, called *pat*

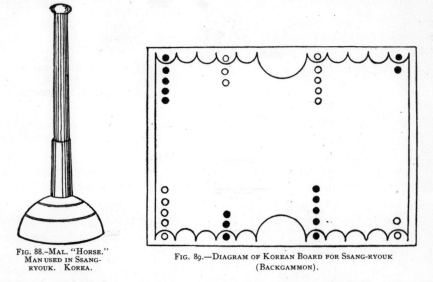

FIG. 88.–MAL. "HORSE."
MAN USED IN SSANG-
RYOUK. KOREA.

FIG. 89.—DIAGRAM OF KOREAN BOARD FOR SSANG-RYOUK
(BACKGAMMON).

(Chinese, *t'in*), "fields," are outlined in black. The large ones in the middle are not counted in moving, and are used to throw the dice in. The men, Fig. 88, are about three and a half inches in height. Fifteen are employed on each side, one set being painted red and the other left the natural color of the wood. They are usually made of boxwood, but some softer wood is used in the cheaper sets. The moves are made according to the throws with two dice, and receive the same names as the corresponding pieces in the Domino game (page 103).

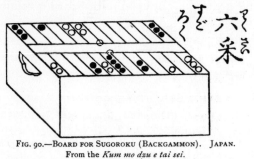

FIG. 90.—BOARD FOR SUGOROKU (BACKGAMMON). JAPAN.
From the *Kum mo dzu e tai sei.*

A diagram of the board, as set at the opening of the game, is shown in Fig. 89. It will be seen to be the same as in the English game of Backgammon. The first player is determined by the highest throw with one die. The pieces are moved as in the English game, but it is customary to move two pieces when doublets are thrown, and doublets do not entitle the player to another

앙모는치놕챵

PLATE XVII.   KOREAN BACKGAMMON.

'throw, nor to an additional count.   A player may take an opponent's place, called *tjap-ta*, "to catch," and the piece so taken must be re-entered again.

When a player gets all, his men around to his own place he b e a r s them off according to his subsequent throws. Plate XVII represents a *kĭ-săing* playing Backgammon with a guest.

The Japanese play Backgammon under the name *Sugoroku* upon a b o a r d, represented in Fig. 90, but the game does not appear to be generally known at the present day.

FIG. 91.—GAISHA PLAYING SUGOROKU.   JAPAN (BOKU-SEN)

Dr. Thomas Hyde describes the Chinese game of Backgammon under

FIG. 92.—CHINESE BACKGAMMON BOARD.   (From Hyde.)

the name of *Çoan kĭ*, which he translates as *erectus ludus*, or *erectorum ludus*, but which might be rendered as the "Bottle game" or "Bottle chess," *Ç o a n* (*tsun*) meaning a vase or bottle and *kĭ* (*k'i*) being a generic term for games played with men or pieces, as chess.[1]

Backgammon is also played in Siam and the Malay Peninsula in much the same manner as in Europe.[2]

The backgammon board may be regarded, without much stretch of the imagination, as the expansion of a circuit like that of the *Nyout* game.

---

[1] "This game is played with dice and small upright pillars, from which the name is derived. The board is divided into eight equal parts by transverse lines, and the pieces, which are from

LXXIV. TJYANG-KEUI—CHESS.

By W. H. Wilkinson, Late H. B. M. Acting Consul-General in Korea.

Korean chess, *Tjyang-keui* (Chinese, *tséung k'i*) is admittedly a variant of Chinese, yet, as will be seen, there are some important differences between the two games. The design of the board, but not its shape, is the same, save that in Korea the files are carried across the " river," which is, in fact, ignored. The men, again, have the same names as in China, and, except that the King is placed in the centre of his " camp," and that the " Horse " and " Elephant " are interchangeable, occupy the same positions at starting. But their powers and privileges in most cases differ largely. A Korean chess-board and men, arranged for a game, is represented in Fig. 93. It will be noticed that the board is not square, but oblong, the width being greater than the breadth. All the Korean chess-boards have this shape, the object in view being to facilitate the moving of pieces when they have reached the opponent's end of the board. It may be observed, in passing, that chess-boards would seem to be all of domestic manufacture, as they are not sold in any shops, even at the capital. The men can be procured,

---

two to three inches high and number sixteen on each side, are arranged upon it when the playing commences, as seen in the figure.

" The pieces are moved line by line, according to the throws with the dice, from the places on the left to the eighth place on the right, and from thence ascending to the opposite side and back to the starting place, the player who first gets all his pieces there winning the game.

" Two dice are thrown, and the pieces are moved to the places which the number of the throw directs. One may move whatever piece or pieces one chooses, according to the number, either pieces which have been moved before or those which have not yet been moved. If, instead of upright pieces, one plays with small flat discs, which is also permitted, they may be placed side by side or piled on top of each other, as seems most convenient.

" A throw of two ' ones ' causes a piece to be set aside and delivered up as lost; or, if the game is played for money, it loses the player the tenth part of his stakes. Whoever throws ' twos ' or ' threes ' begins moving to the second or third lines, and so on. If doublets are thrown, one may move to the place corresponding to the half number of such doublets; and this may be done by moving one piece once to such half number, or two pieces at the same time to the place corresponding with such whole number, for in this case either one piece or two pieces together may be moved. If ' five ' and ' six,' which make eleven, are thrown, one may move one piece to the fifth place and another to the eleventh; or else move two pieces at the same time to the tenth line or place; and then one of them to the next line, which is the eleventh. And thus with respect to other throws: if single (as ' two ' and ' four '), for the single numbers move as many places, but if joined (as ' five ' and ' six ') then otherwise, as already stated." *De Ludis Orientalibus*, Oxford, 1694, p. 65.

[2] See author's paper on *Chinese Games with Dice and Dominoes*. Report U. S. National Museum, 1893.

PLATE XVIII.   KOREAN CHESS.

though they are usually made to order, inclosed in a net resembling an onion bag.

Another feature in which the Korean game will be seen to differ outwardly from the Chinese is the shape of the men and the circumstances that the hieroglyphics on one side are inscribed in the "grass character," or running hand. Korean chessmen are not circular, as in China, but octagonal,[1] and vary in size according to their value, the King (General) being the largest, the Chariot, Elephant, Horse and Cannon of medium

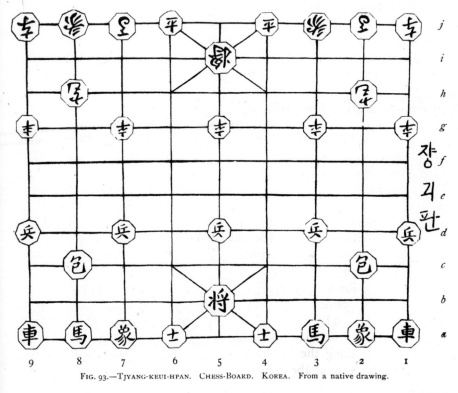

FIG. 93.—TJVANG-KEUI-HPAN. CHESS-BOARD. KOREA. From a native drawing.

size and the Pawns (soldiers) and Counsellors the smallest. The hieroglyphs on one side are usually colored red, on the other green—the draughtsmen, for such in appearance they are, being all of the same wood and undyed.

---

[1] The men of the set exhibited by the Korean Government at the Columbian Exposition, Chicago, now in the Museum of the University of Pennsylvania, are circular, but vary in size according to their value. The two sets in the U. S. National Museum, Washington, are octagonal.

In describing the powers of the pieces, it will be convenient to give each its corresponding Western name, the *Hpo*, a piece we unfortunately lack, being styled a Cannon. The Korean names are as follows:

1. *Tjyang* (Chinese, *tsáung*), "General," more usually called *Koung* (Chinese, *kún*), "Palace," the King.
2. *Tcha* (Chinese, *kü*), "Chariot," Rook.
3. *Hpo* (Chinese), *p'áu*), "Cannon."
4. *Pyeng* (Chinese, *ping*), or *tjol* (Chinese, *tsut*), "Foot-soldier," Pawn.
5. *Sà* (Chinese, *sz'*), "Counsellor," Queen.
6. *Syang* (Chinese, *tséung*), "Elephant," Bishop.
7. *Ma* (Chinese, *má*), "Horse," Knight.

The moves of these pieces follow two general laws, the existence of which makes Korean chess a more finished or more logical game than the Chinese. The first is that the pieces invariably take as they move; the second, that, within their limitations, they move along any marked line. In Chinese chess the *P'áu* moves like a Rook, but takes only when a piece intervenes; the Korean Cannon moves and takes in the same way. On the Chinese board the files between the fifth and sixth ranks are not marked, in order to better indicate the "river," after the crossing of which the Pawns acquire increased powers; yet for the purposes of play they exist. The diagonal lines joining the corners of the General's "camp" may be, though they seldom are, omitted from a Chinese chess-board; but neither they nor the river files must be left out on the Korean. For, as has been said, wherever a line is marked a Korean piece can, within its limitations, move along it. Thus the Chariot, which has precisely the same powers as our Rook, may move from one corner of the "camp" to the centre, or, if so desired, to the corner diagonally opposite, because those points are connected by a marked line. For the same reason the Cannon, if on one such corner, may, when the centre is occupied, hop over to the opposite corner along the line of the diagonal. A similar train of reasoning has made identical the movements of the two Counsellors and the General.

The General, or King, as he shall be called, may move from his original position at the centre on to any one of the nine points in his camp, but he can never leave his camp. Within it he moves only one step at a time, and that only along marked lines. Thus, if the King were at 5 a he could move thence to 5 b (the centre), 6 a or 4 a, but he could not move to 4 b or 6 b, because there is no line connecting 5 a with these last two points. As in the Chinese game, the Kings check one another across the board if they are on the same file, with no piece intervening. Korean chess, however, leans here, as in other games, toward the losing side. If

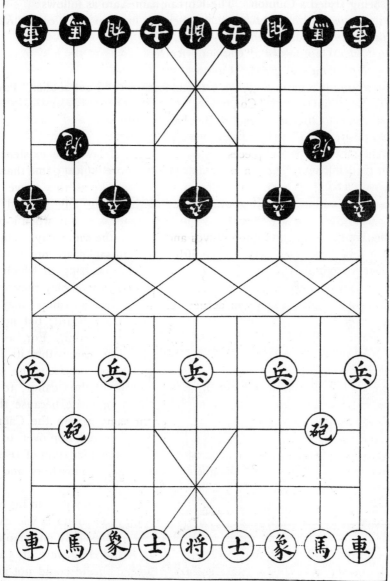

FIG. 94.—TSÉUNG K'I PÁN. CHESS-BOARD. CHINA.

one of the players has an overpowering advantage the other is allowed, should opportunity occur, to check his opponent's King with his own.

Thus, if Red has King on 6 i, Pawns on 3 d and 6 d, while Green has King on 5 a, Rook on 7 a, Pawn on 7 d, Red is allowed to play King 6 i to 5 i (check). When Green moves his King to 4 a or 6 a (his only alternatives), Red again checks with his King, making the game a draw. It should, however, be observed that the act of checking the opponent's King with one's own is in itself a confession of inferiority, and deprives the player of any chance of winning the game,—he can at most draw it.[1]

The King on the losing side is allowed yet another privilege. If he is the only piece on his side, and if his moving would greatly endanger him, he is allowed, as the equivalent of a move, to turn over and remain in his original position. Thus (the finish of an actual game, played in the British Legation garden at Seoul):

Red: King on 5 i, Queen on 4 i, Pawn on 5 c, Knight on 3 c.

Green: King on 4 b.

Green's only move—K 4 b to 4 a—would be followed by Red—Pawn 5 c to 5 b, mate. Green therefore being called on to play, simply turned over his King. The game then proceeded:

RED.	GREEN.
Kt 4 d to 5 f	K 4 b to 4 a
Kt 5 b to 6 d	K 4 a to 4 b
Pawn 5 c to 5 b, mate.	

Instead of playing K 4 b to 4 a in reply to the move of the Red Knight, Green might again have reversed the King, for there is no limit to this exercise.

The Counsellors, or Queens, move in all respects like the King, and are equally confined to the nine points of the camp. They cannot give

---

[1] The same penalty attaches to the checking of the opponent's King by a piece which the King could capture were it not on an open file of his rival's. Thus:

Red: King on 4 j, Knight on 3 c, Pawn on 4 b.

Green: King on 5 a, Rook on 1 i, Bishop on 1 j.

If it is Red's turn to play he mates by Pawn to 5 b, for if the King moves to 6 b he is equally under check by the Pawn, since the points 5 b and 6 a are connected by a marked line. If it is Green's turn he can only play R 1 i to 5 i, *a draw, not a mate.*

A player cannot force a draw by checking his opponent's King with his own, even though the alternative is to be mated if he has a greater strength in men. For example:

Red: King on 6 j, Queen on 5 j, Bishop on 5 i, Kt on 3 c, Pawn on 4 c.

Green: King on 5 a, Rook on 1 g, Cannon on 1 f, Kt on 3 g, Pawn on 3 f.

Red would mate by Pawn to 5 b, but if it is Green's turn, he may not play King 5 a to 6 a, check and draw, because the value of his pieces is superior to that of Red's, a Rook and a Cannon being worth more than a Queen and a Bishop.

check, however, across the board. They are more powerful than the Chinese *Sz'*, which can only occupy the five points on the diagonals.

The Chariots, or Rooks, have exactly the powers of our own Castles, or the Chinese *Kü*, except that, as has been said, they can also move along the marked diagonals of either their own or the enemy's camp.

The Horses (Knights) have precisely the move of the Chinese *Má*, which is also that of the Western Knight, with one important limitation. The Korean and the Chinese *Má* always moves first one step along a file or rank, and then a step diagonally. If there be a piece, whether of his own side or the enemy's, at the elbow, so to speak, of his beat, he cannot move. Thus in the example given above, the Red Knight on 3 c could not move to 5 b or 5 d, because of the Pawn on 4 c; had the Pawn been on 4 b or 4 d the Knight would not be estopped. It will be seen that it is, owing to this rule, possible to cover check from a Korean Knight.

The Elephant, or Bishop, moves one step along a rank or file, then two steps diagonally. It differs from the *Jamal* or Camel of Tamerlane's Chess, in that the latter moves first a step diagonally, and then two straightwise, and has, which the *Syang* has not, the privilege of vaulting. For the Korean Elephant must have a clear course from start to finish, like the Chinese Elephant. Unlike the latter (whose move is that of Tamerlane's *Fil*, or the original Bishop, the *Fil* less their power of vaulting), the Korean Elephant is not confined to its own side of the river, but may move freely all over the board.

At starting, the Korean Bishop must stand on one of the two points between the Rook and the Queen, the Knight being placed on the other; but on which point depends upon the whim of the player. Perhaps it would be simpler to say that at the commencement of the game, the men being arranged as in Chinese chess (except that the Kings are on 5 b, not 5 a, and 5 i, not 5 j, either player may, before moving, but not afterward, interchange Knight or Bishop at one or both sides of his line. If one player so interchanges, it is generally considered advisable for the other to do the same, but he is under no obligation in the matter.

The Soldiers (Pawns) differ from those of China in that they have from the first the move which the Chinese *Ping* only gets after crossing the river. A Korean Pawn moves one step sideways or forward, but never backward or diagonally. When he reaches his tenth rank (the enemy's first) he does not change his condition, but remains a Pawn, restricted to a sidelong movement up and down that rank. For this reason a Pawn is not often advanced to the last line—is, indeed, seldom carried beyond the eighth rank, his strongest position. We have seen that, in common with the Rook, the King, and Queen, the Pawn can travel along the diagonal of the camp.

The Cannon differs from the *P'áu* of China in that it moves as it takes, and that another Cannon can neither form a "Screen" for it nor be taken by it. The Korean *Hpo* moves in a straight line, horizontally or perpendicularly, but only when some piece (not itself a Cannon) intervenes. Thus, in the example above given, the Cannon on 1 f can move to 1 h, 1 i or 1 j over the Rook on 1 g, or to 4 b, 5 f . . . 8 f over the Pawn on 3 f. If moved to 1 j it would give check to the enemy's King on 6 j, because the Queen on 5 j intervening forms a Screen. But as the men are placed at the commencement of the game, the Cannon on 2 c cannot take the Knight on 2 j, because the other Cannon on 2 h does not act as a Screen. Although this is the case, an intervening Cannon is not altogether ignored. For instance, if Red had had a Cannon on 4 a when Green checked by Cannon 1 f to 1 j, he could have replied by Cannon 4 a to 4 j, interposing, when the Green Cannon on 1 j would practically bear on nothing but the empty points 1 f to 1 a. This restriction of the power of the Cannon makes it inferior to the Chinese *P'áu* and its movements more cumbrous. In all other respects the Korean game is a distinct advance on the Chinese, and, this drawback modified, might even aspire to rivalry with Western Chess were the King and Queens permitted to move freely over the board.

There are, as far as can be learnt, no native books whatsoever on the subject of Korean Chess corresponding with the work which formed the basis of the writer's *Manual of Chinese Chess.*[1] Nor have the numerous books of end games or problems of China any counterpart in Korea. Chess in the latter country is regarded, in spite of its unusual diffusion, as a somewhat frivolous pastime, suitable for young persons and rustics. The educated Korean, deeply imbued as he is with Chinese sympathies, affects to prefer *Pa-tok* (No. LXXV), though it is open to considerable doubt whether he would not, as a matter of actual fact, rather play at chess.

The first move is usually conceded to the weaker player, a plain proof that the advantage is supposed to rest with the opener. The usual commencement is either a Rook's Pawn horizontally or a Knight interposing between the Cannons to serve as a Screen for one of them. In the following short game the Bishops were placed on 3 a, 8 a, 2 j, and 7 j respectively:

---

[1] *A Manual of Chinese Chess.* Shanghai: Printed at the *North China Herald* office, 1893.

RED.	GREEN.
1. P 9 g to 8 g	1. P 1 d to 2 d
2. Kt 3 j to 4 h	2. Kt 7 a to 6 c
To form screen for Cannon.	
3. B 2 j to 5 h	3. C 8 c to 5 c
4. Kt 8 j to 7 h	4. P 5 d to 4 d
To defend Pawn on 5 g.	Brings Cannon to bear on Bishop.
5. Kt 4 h to 5 f	5. B 3 a to 5 d
Green Cannon now bears on Pawn.	Threatens Pawn on 3 g.
6. P 3 g to 4 g	6. Kt 2 a to 4 b
7. Kt 5 i to 5 j	7. B 8 a to 6 d
8. R 9 j to 9 f	8. R 1 a to 1 e
9. Q 4 j to 5 i	9. R 1 e to 4 e
10. P 1 g to 2 g (?)	10. P 9 d to 9 e
11. R 9 f to 6 f	11. P 9 e to 8 e
12. C 8 h to 6 h	12. R 9 a to 9 j
13. B 7 j to 9 g	13. C 2 c takes P 2 g
14. R 1 j to 1 b	14. C 5 c to 7 c
15. C 6 h to 3 h	15. P 8 e to 7 e
16. C 3 h to 3 b (check)	16. K 5 b to 5 a
17. C 3 b to 3 i	17. P 7 e to 7 f
	Better to 6 e
18. P 7 g takes P 7 f	18. C 2 g to 2 c
19. C 3 i to 3 a (check)	19. Q 4 a to 5 b
20. R 1 b to 1 a	20. Kt 4 b to 2 a
21. R 1 a takes Kt 2 a	21. B 5 d takes C 3 a
22. R 2 a takes B 3 a (check)	22. Q 5 b to 4 a
23. Kt 5 f takes B 6 d	23. P 7 d takes Kt 6 d
24. R 6 f takes P 6 d	24. C 7 c takes Kt 7 h
25. R 6 d takes Kt 6 c	25. Q 6 a to 6 b
26. R 6 c to 8 c	26. C 7 h to 7 b
27. R 8 c to 8 a (check)	27. Q 6 b to 6 a
28. B 9 g to 7 d (check)	28. K 5 a to 5 b
	Only move.
29. R 3 a takes Q 4 a (check)	29. K 5 b takes R 4 a
30. R 8 a takes Q 6 a (mate)	

"Check" in Korean is *tjyang*, "General" (King), and "mate," *tjyou-sa*." [1]

---

[1] Mr. Wilkinson is to be credited with the first publication by any Western writer on Korean Chess. See his *Chess in Korea* in the *Pall Mall Budget*, Dec. 27th, 1894.—S. C.

Plate XVIII represents two men playing chess. The one on the right wears the hat such as is worn in doors, which marks him as the host, while the other is doubtless a guest. In Plate XIX the players are both in indoor dress, the one on the right being distinguished by his hat as an official.

In Japan, the game of chess is called *Shogi* (Chinese, *tséung k'i*), Fig. 95, and although in general the same, differs in many particulars from the

Chinese and Korean game. It is played on a board, usually in the form of a small table, like that used for *Go*, with nine squares on a side. The men are placed on the squares, not on the intersections, as in China. They consist of punt-shaped pieces of wood of different sizes, lying flat on the board and slightly inclined toward the front,

FIG. 95.—SHOGI. CHESS. JAPAN (BOKU-SEN).

the direction of the point determining to whom the piece belongs. Unlike other games of chess, the men are all of one color, and the same pieces serve for the player and his adversary. Another peculiarity is that any piece taken up may be entered by the adversary in any place he chooses and at any time he thinks desirable, such entry constituting his move. The pieces, of which there are twenty on each side, are as follows:

O Shō, " General," commonly called *O* (1) = King. *Kin Shō*, " Gold Generals," commonly called *Kin* (2). *Gin Shō*, " Silver Generals," commonly called *Gin* (2). *Hisha*, " Flying Wagon," (1) = Castle. *Kakkō*, " Angle going," commonly called *Kaku* (1) = Bishop. *Keima*,[1] (2) = Knights. *Kyōsha*, " Fragrant Chariots,"[2] (2). *Hōhei*, " Foot-soldiers," commonly called *Fu* (9) = Pawns.

The *O Shō*, or " General," stands in the centre of the first row. He moves one square in any direction, and loses the game when checkmated. The " Gold Generals " stand on either side of the King, and move one square in any direction, except the two back diagonals.

---

[1] Written with the Chinese characters *kwai má*, which may be translated " Honorable Horse."

[2] *Kyōsha* is sometimes written with the Chinese characters *king kü*, " Capital Chariot," instead of *héung kü*, " Fragrant Chariot."

PLATE XIX.   KOREAN CHESS.

The " Silver Generals " stand on each side next to the " Gold Generals,"
and move one square in any direction, except sideways and backward. The
Keima stand next to the " Silver Generals," and have our Knight's move,
but only forward. The *Kyōsha* occupy the extreme ends and move any
number of squares, perpendicularly only. The *Hisha* stand in front of the
right-hand *Keima* and has the move of our Castle. The *Kakkō* stand in
front of the left-hand *Keima*, and have the move of our Bishop. The
" Foot-soldiers," or Pawns, occupy the third row, and move and take one
square forward only.

The three rows nearest each side constitute the opposing camps. The
King and " Gold Generals " retain their rank unchanged throughout the
game, but the following pieces are promoted, immediately upon entering the
enemy's camp, when they are turned over, then new names being written
on their reverse sides. The *Hisha* becomes *Ryo-wo*, " Dragon King," and
has the privilege, in addition to its former power, of moving one square
diagonally like the *Kakkō*. The *Kakkō* becomes *Ryo-ma*, " Dragon Horse,"
and has the additional power of moving one square forward, sideways, or
backward. The " Silver Generals," *Keima*, *Kyōsha*, and *Hohei*, or Pawns,
can all attain the rank of " Gold Generals." A detailed account of *Shogi*
will be found in Mr. Falkener's *Games, Ancient and Oriental*, from which
the above account was extracted. The *Wa Kan san sai dzu e* states that
the date of the origin of the game is unknown.

LXXV. PA-TOK—PEBBLE GAME.

The Korean game of *Pa-tok* is practically identical with the Chinese
game of *Wai k'i* (Wei ch'i), which is played in Japan under the name of *Go*.
It is played by two players upon a board special to the game, and with two
sets of men of different colors. " The board is divided into squares like a
chess-board, but into a much greater number, and without any alternation of
color, their total number being 324, 18x18. This, however, does not represent the scale of the game, because, as in Chinese chess, the pieces are
played on the intersection of the horizontal and vertical lines and not on
their intervals. Thus, as there are nineteen lines in either direction, the total
number of places on which the men can be played is 19x19, or 361."

The Korean board, *pa-tok-hpan*, differs from that of Japan, in being
made in the form of a small hollow table, while the Japanese board consists
of a solid block of wood. The Korean board is resonant, and by an
arrangement of wires stretched within, emits a musical note when a piece is

played. A specimen in the Museum of the University of Pennsylvania, Fig. 96, is eleven inches high and about sixteen inches square.

In China, the boards are printed on paper, with the printer's name attached, so as to be ready for either playing or scoring a game, and there is a margin at the top for writing remarks, such as noting a point from which a pip of one color has been taken up, and into which a piece of another color has subsequently been played.[1]

FIG. 96.—PA-TOK-HPAN. BOARD FOR PEBBLE GAME. KOREA. Museum of Archæology, Univ. of Penna. No. 16,431.

The men used in Korea are small, polished black pebbles, *mak-tjă* (Chinese, *hak tsz'*), and irregular pieces of polished white shell, *păik-tjă* (Chinese, *pák tsz'*). The set in the University Museum consists of 143 black and 140 white pieces,[2] contained, as is customary, in two unpainted wooden bowls with wooden covers, called *pa-tok-htong* (Chinese, *t'ung*).

In Japan the men, *go ishi*, are known as *kuro-ishi*, "black," and *shiro-ishi*, "white stones," and are slightly convex discs about seven-eighths of an inch in diameter. Those in the same museum consist, respectively, of worked slate and shell, and are contained in black-lacquered wooden boxes with covers.

"The Chinese, in the books which treat of the game, divide the board

---

[1] Z. Volpicelli, *Journal of the China Branch of the Royal Asiatic Society*, Vol. XXVI, p. 80, Shanghai, 1894.

[2] These do not appear to be the requisite number.

PLATE XX. KOREAN PA-TOK GAME.

into four equal parts, which they call 'corners' (*kok* or *ü*), and which are called by the names of the four Chinese tones:

P'*ing* for the lower left corner.
Shé*ung* for the upper left corner.
.Hü for the upper right corner.
Yap for the lower right corner.

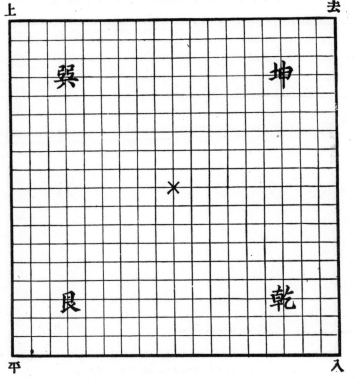

FIG. 97.—DIAGRAM OF WAI K'I BOARD, SHOWING METHOD OF DIVIDING. (From Volpicelli.)

" In each of these four sections a place is generally marked out **at** a distance of four steps along the principal diagonal counted from the outer
angle. Each spot is, therefore, equi-distant from the two external sides of
the section. These four points are called *Kan*, *Sun*, *Kw'an*, and *K'in*, and the
players generally begin the game by alternately covering them, each player
occupying two at opposite angles. Sometimes the centre of the board is
marked."

The Korean board is marked in the same manner, with the addition of eight intermediary marks as shown in Fig. 98.

The Chinese have adopted a system of notation for each of the four corners. This is minutely described by Mr. Volpicelli, to whose treatise the reader is referred for particulars. Fig. 99, upon which a few spots are marked with the numbers used to designate their position, will give a general idea.

" The players place their men alternately on any of the points of inter-

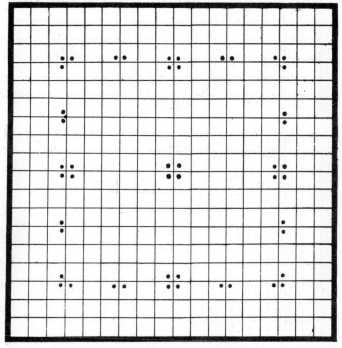

FIG. 98.—FACE OF KOREAN BOARD FOR PA-TOK.

section of the horizontal and vertical lines not already occupied," the object of the game being to occupy as much of the board as possible, victory being decided in favor of the player who has command of the most spots. "Space can be occupied in two ways—by placing men on the different points, and by forming an enclosure with one's men, the space thus contained being reckoned as one's territory." The latter gives the name of the game, *Wai* (to surround) being its principal object. The simplest possible enclosure that can be formed on the board is that of four men enclosing one spot, which is called in Chinese, *ngán*, " eye;" in Japanese, *me*, having the same meaning, and in Korean, *tjïp*, " house," and which can be seen in the lower left-hand corner of Fig. 100. The next in simplicity is that formed by six men enclosing two spots, an example of which is given in the lower right-hand corner of the same diagram. In the same way large enclosures can ᵕbe formed with a greater number of men, as will be seen in the upper left-

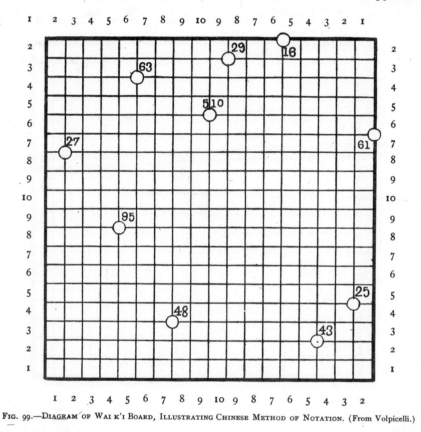

FIG. 99.—DIAGRAM OF WAI K'I BOARD, ILLUSTRATING CHINESE METHOD OF NOTATION. (From Volpicelli.)

hand corner of Fig. 100. All enclosures require a smaller number of men to form them when they are situated around a corner or angle of the board, as then only two sides need be formed, the other two being the limits of the board itself. All enclosures may be formed not only round unoccupied spots, but also round unprotected men of the adversary, who are forthwith taken and their empty places become the conqueror's territory. The element of strife thus comes in and lends interest to the game. The interest is not concentrated in one spot, as at chess, around the King, but is diffused all over the board, as every single spot is equally important in effecting the result and counts in the grand total which represents the position of each side at the end of the struggle.

An opponent's pieces may be captured when they are completely surrounded, but whenever a group of men contains within itself two or more empty spots forming complete eyes, it is secure against attack. It does not

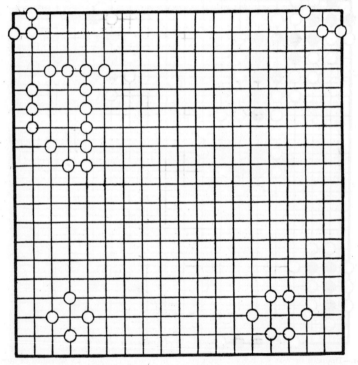

FIG. 100.—DIAGRAM OF WAI K'I BOARD, SHOWING EYES AND ENCLOSURES. (From Volpicelli.)

matter where or how far apart from each other these eyes are situated, provided they form part of one unbroken group of men joined together. The upper left-hand corner of Fig. 101 exhibits a territory which cannot be conquered by the adversary, because it contains three complete eyes, any two of which alone would be sufficient to secure its independence. If White should fill up an eye at any point, Black in his turn would take the man that White played, for it would be surrounded by his men.

A detailed account of these enclosures is given by Mr. Volpicelli, who describes the manner in which they may be joined together to secure them against attack. At the close of the game there may be empty spaces, surrounded partly with white and partly with black pieces, so that neither side can claim them. In such cases they are alternately filled up by the two players before the counting begins. Each player then counts his pieces, including the eyes which he has surrounded, and the one having the highest wins the game.

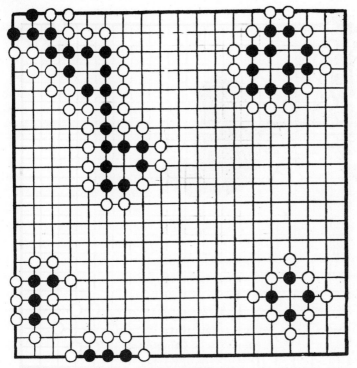

FIG. 101.—DIAGRAM OF WAI K'I BOARD, SHOWING PROTECTED ENCLOSURES AND METHODS OF ATTACK.
(From Volpicelli.)

The *Wa Kan san sai dzu e* gives the following account of the game of *Go*, which it states is also called *Za in*[1] (Chinese, *tso yan*), so named by Wang Chung Long, of Tsin,[2] and *Shu dan*[3] (Chinese, *shau t'ám*), so named by Chi Kung, of Tsin.[4] The board is called *go ban* (Chinese, *k'i kuk*). The boxes for the stones are called *go ki* (Chinese, *k'i lim*).

The Kwáng po wuh chi[1] says that a subject of Kieh named Wu Ts'au invented *Go* and gambling. It is also said that the Emperor Yao (B. C. 2356) invented *Go* and taught it to his son, Tan Chu.

Another says that the Emperor Shun (B. C. 2255) invented *Go* and taught it to his son, Shang Kiun, who was ignorant.

The *go ban no me*,[2] literally the " eyes of chess-board," are painted with lacquer. There are nineteen each way, vertically and horizontally. The *Go* stones, white and black, together number 360, corresponding with the number of days of the year. The nine stars correspond with the Nine Lights of Heaven,[3] the sun and moon and the seven stars of the constellation *Tau* (Ursa Major).

FIG. 102.—THE GAME OF GO. JAPAN. (BOKU-SEN.)

It is written in the Wú Ts'ah Tsú that among the playthings of modern and ancient times there is nothing more remote than *Go*. Next to wine and women, it leads men astray. If they think it difficult, even village boys and common people can play it very skillfully ; but if it be thought very easy, even the wisest and most intelligent, though they investigate it through generations, may not acquire it correctly. It is recorded in the I King, written by Chun, of Hántán, that the *Go* board had 17 vertical and 17 horizontal lines, making 289 ways, which is 71 ways less than the present board. The writer adds, " I think before the Han and Wei dynasties (206 B. C.–265 A. D.) all were like this."

The Sz' king tsáh kí[4] says that Tú Fu Tsz',[5] of Tú Ling, played *Go*

---

[1] A cyclopedia in fifty books by Tùng Sze-chang, who brought it to a conclusion in 1607. A. Wylie, *Notes on Chinese Literature*, London, 1867, p. 150.

[2] Written in the Chinese text with a character called in Chinese *kwá*, compounded of *sz'*, " four," and *kwá*, " diagrams," evidently referring to the four diagrams indicating the Four Directions (see p. 93).

[3] *Chinese Reader's Manual*, Pt. II, No. 292.

[4] The Sz' king tsáh kí (Se king tsä ke) in six books, is a record of incidents at Ch'áng-gan, the metropolis during the Han dynasty, being supplementary to Pan Koó's history. By some this has been attributed to Lêw Hin, of the Han, and by others to Kŏ Húng, of the Tsin ; but the probability is in favor of Woô Yun, of the sixth century, being the author.—A. Wylie, *Notes on Chinese Literature*, p. 151.

[5] A. D. 712–770. A celebrated poet, contemporary with and second only to Li Peh. He was

well, and became the first under heaven. Wú Yen Wú, commonly called Tsz' K'ing, of Ts'ien T'áng ; Láng Yé, of Nán Sung, and Wang Hi, were the first of their times.

P'áu P'oh Tsz'[1] says that the most skillful player was called *K'i shing* (that is, " Chess Sage "), therefore Yen Tsz' K'ing (Wú Yen Wú) and Má Sui Ming are called Chess Sages even at present. One who carves skill-fully is called *Muk shing*, or " Wood Sage," therefore Chang Hêng[2] and Má Chung are known as *Muk Shing*.

In the time of T'ai Chung, of the T'ang dynasty (A. D. 847–860) Japan sent a tribute of *Go* stones made of gems to China, saying that in the south of that country there is an island called Shiu Ken (Chinese, *tsáp in*), on which is a pond called Shudan (Chinese, *shau t'ám*). In it the *Go* stones are produced. The Japanese commentator says the island of Shiu Ken is not known ; it may be Nachi no hama, in Kishiū.

The board for *Go* is about six inches (Japanese[3]) thick, one foot four inches long, and one foot three inches wide. The rectangles are eight-tenths by seven-tenths of an inch. Each direction has 19 *me* (or " eyes "). The best wood is *Kaya*[4] (Chinese, *fi*); the next, *Hinoki*[5] (Chinese, *kúi*), and the next best, *Katsura*[6] (Chinese, *kwai*). When a new board of *Kaya* wood cracks, if it is put in a box for some time it becomes as before.

Tradition says that Lord Kibi introduced *Go* into Japan in the 7th year of *Ten Pei* (A. D. 735), he having been twenty years in China. Some say Shaku Ben Shō went to China to study, and played *Go* with Hüan Tsung

---

a native of Tú Ling, and is, consequently, referred to under this pseudonym. High honors were lavished upon him during his lifetime, in recognition no less of his learning than of his poetical genius.—*Chinese Reader's Manual*, No. 680.

[1] The adopted designation of Ko Hung, fourth century A. D. One of the most celebrated among the doctors of Taoism and adepts in the art and practice of alchemy.—*Chinese Reader's Manual*, No. 274.

[2] A. D. 78–139. Grand Historiographer in the reign of Han Shun Ti, and celebrated for his universal knowledge, but more particularly for his mastery of astronomical science. He constructed an uranosphere, and greatly advanced the sciences of astronomy and mathematics among his countrymen.—*Chinese Reader's Manual*, No. 13.

[3] The Japanese foot is about $\frac{4}{1000}$ths shorter than ours, but the inches are longer, being tenths instead of twelfths of a foot.

[4] The *Torreya Nucifera*, a species of yew, commonly called Fetid Yew, because the young foliage when bruised emits a disagreeable odor.

[5] The *Thuya Obtusa*, a species of cedar.

[6] The *Cercidiphyllum Japonica*, a tree related to the American Magnolia. From this wood the Ainos hollow their canoes and make mortars found in every Aino house and used in pounding grain.—Charles S. Sargent, *Garden and Forest*, Vol. VI, p. 52.

(reigned A. D. 713–756) before he became Emperor. The writer remarks that perhaps Ben Shō already knew the game.

Japanese annals relate that in the 7th month of the 10th year of *Ten Pei* (A. D. 738) Otomo no Shukune Komushi played *Go* with Nakatomi no Miya Dokoro no Muragi Adzumabito in the leisure time of office, when a dispute arose and Komushi insulted Adzumabito and killed him with his sword.

In the records of the Empress Jitō (A. D. 690–696) there is a decree prohibiting the game of *Sugoroku* (p. 81). Perhaps *Go* existed in Japan before this, but it is not known when it began.

Among the most skillful players were I Un Rōnin in the time of the Emperor Go-Tsuchimikado (A. D. 1465–1500); Hon In Bō and Nikkai Hō In, of Jakkōji, in the time of the Emperor Goyōzei (A. D. 1587–1611).

At present Hon In Bō is called the "Chess Sage." During his life he received an annuity. At the present day a man named Hon In Bō Dō Saku is the expert of all time, and may be called the "Go Sage."

The game of *Go* is extremely popular in Japan at the present time, and is much played by military men, who regard it as an exercise in military tactics and instructive in the art of war.

A clue to the meaning of the game of *Wai k'i*, or *Go*, is found in the analysis of the Chinese name *kwá* (Japanese, *kei*) applied to the squares of the board. As already stated, it is compounded of the Chinese characters *sz'*, four, and *kwá*, the diagrams used in divination. The four diagrams referred to, as will be seen from Fig. 97, are those called *Kan*, *Sun*, *Kw'an*, and *K'in*, and designate the North East, South East, South West, and North West. Thus it appears, like *Nyout* and *Pachisi*, to be regarded as a game of the Four Directions, and the board has the same cosmical significance as is discovered to underly all other boards upon which games are played. An agreement is also found between the quarters of the board and the four tones of the Chinese spoken language. This correlation appears to be practically extended in the Korean board to the notes of the musical scale, the board emitting a musical note when a piece is played. The note of the board in the University Museum corresponds with F, first space, treble clef, of the European scale.

LXXVI. OU-MOUL-KO-NO—WELL KONO.

The games played on diagrams, like our game of Merrells, receive the name of *Ko-no* in Korea, a term my informant could not further define.

Similar games are known as *K'i*[1] in China, the name which is applied there to games played upon boards, as, for example, *Tséung k'i*, " Chess," and *Wai k'i*.

Black and white stones are used in these games, which receive the

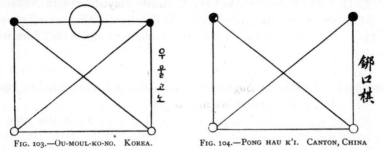

<table>
<tr><td>FIG. 103.—OU-MOUL-KO-NO. KOREA.</td><td>FIG. 104.—PONG HAU K'I. CANTON, CHINA</td></tr>
</table>

same names in Korea, China, and Japan as those used in the game of *Pa-tok* (No. LXXV), *Wai k'i*, and *Go*.

In all games of *Kono*, as in *Pa-tok*, the black men move first.

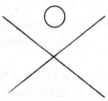

Ou-moul-ko-no is played upon a diagram, Fig. 103. Each player has two stones which they may put down alternately or may set at the beginning, as shown on the diagram. The players move one piece at a time, in alternate plays along the sides of the square, except that marked with a circle, which is barred, or from the corners to the centre. The object of the game is to block the opponent's men so that they cannot move.

FIG. 105.—SUA TOK TONG. SIAM.

The game of *Ou-moul-ko-no* is called *Pong hau k'i* in China (*Kwang-tung*), and is played upon a diagram like Fig. 104.

In Siam a similar game is played upon a diagram represented by Fig. 105, and is called *Sua tok tong*.

LXXVII. NEI-PAT-KO-NO—FOUR-FIELD KONO.

Each player has eight pieces, which are set as shown in Fig. 106. The players move alternately along the lines and take an opponent's piece by jumping over one of their own pieces to the third place. When not thus taking, the pieces are moved one square at a time. The object is to block or capture the opponent's men.

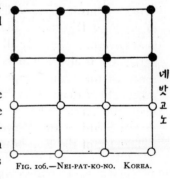

FIG. 106.—NEI-PAT-KO-NO. KOREA.

---

[1] This name apparently refers to the men, stone or wood, with which the game is played, and not to the board or diagram.

LXXVIII. O-PAT-KO-NO—FIVE-FIELD KONO.

The board is set as shown in Fig. 107. The players move one square at a time, either backward or forward, diagonally across the squares. The

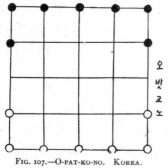

object of the game is to get the pieces across to the other side in the place of those of the opponent, and the one who does this first wins the game.

FIG. 107.—O-PAT-KO-NO. KOREA.

LXXIX. RYOUK-PAT-KO-NO—SIX-FIELD KONO.

This game was only known by name to my informants, who were not familiar with the method of play.

LXXX. KON-TJIL—MERRELLS.

The familiar game of Merrells is known in Korea under the name of *Kon-tjül.*

In China it is called *Sám k'i,* or "Three Chess," Fig. 108, and is played as follows : Each of the two players alternately puts down a piece upon one of the twenty-four points on the board. The object is to get three in a row, and when a player gets three pieces in a line he marks one of his opponent's men as dead by putting one of his own men on top of it. When all the twenty-four points on the board are occupied, the "dead" pieces are removed and the players move in turn, one space at a time. When a player succeeds in getting three of his pieces in a line he takes one of his opponent's. The game continues until one wins, either by taking the other's men or blocking them so that they cannot move.

I am told by a Chinese merchant that this game was invented by Chao Kw'ang-yin,[1] A. D. 917–975, the founder of the Sung dynasty.

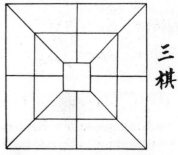

FIG. 108.—SÁM K'I. CANTON, CHINA.

LXXXI. KOL-HPAI, BONE TABLETS—DOMINOES.

The Koreans call dominoes *Kol-hpai* (Chinese, *kwat p'ái*), "Bone tablets," or *Hó-hpai* (Chinese, *ú p'ái*), "Foreign tablets." The latter is said to be the more correct name, and is also applied to a particular game played with dominoes.

---

[1] *Chinese Reader's Manual,* No. 47.

A set consists of 21 different pieces, 11 of which are duplicated, making 32 pieces in the complete set, as in the Chinese game, Fig. 109. They differ from European dominoes, Fig. 110, in the absence of the blanks. A set of Korean dominoes from Seoul in the United States National Museum, Washington, is made of ivory, and numbers 32 pieces. They measure $\frac{3}{4} \times \frac{7}{16} \times \frac{3}{16}$ inches, and are marked with incised spots. The "one" and "four" spots are painted red and all the others black, and the one spots are much larger than the others and very deeply incised. The 32 dominoes are paired, as shown in Fig. 111: 1–1 1–1, 1–2 4–5, 2–2 2–2, 1–3 1–3, 3–3 3–3, 1–4 2–3, 2–4 3–4, 4–4 4–4, 1–5 1–5, 2–5 3–5, 5–5 5–5, 1–6 1–6, 2–6 3–6, 4–6 4–6, 5–6 5–6, 6–6 6–6. Those of which there are two are mated with each other, and those of which there are but one with reference to the sum of the spots, but not in the manner of the Chinese series, Fig. 116. The pieces

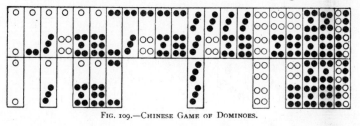

FIG. 109.—CHINESE GAME OF DOMINOES.

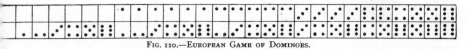

FIG. 110.—EUROPEAN GAME OF DOMINOES.

receive the same names as those given the dice throws in the game of *Ssang-ryouk* (No. LXXIII), viz.:

1–1, *syo-syo*, "smallest."	3–3, *tjyang-sam*, "long three."
1–2, *tjoui-hko*, "rat nose."	3–4, *sam-să*, "three, four."
1–3, *syo-sam*, "small, three."	3–5, *sam-o*, "three, five."
1–4, *păik-să*, "white, four."	3–6, *sam-ryouk*, "three, six."
1–5, *păik-i*, "white, five."	4–4, *tjoun-hong*, "superior red."
1–6, *păik-ryouk*, "white, six."	4–5, *să-o*, "four, five."
2–2, *tjoun-a*, "superior two."	4–6, *să-ryouk*, "four, six."
2–3, *a-sam*, "two, three."	5–5, *tjoun-o*, "superior five."
2–4, *a-să*, "two, four."	5–6, *o-ryouk*, "five, six."
2–5, *koan-i*, "sovereign two."	6–6, *tjoun-ryouk*, "superior six."
2–6, *a-ryouk*, "two, six."	

Dominoes are regarded as a vulgar game in Korea. They are used in gambling, and are not much played as a social game by the highest classes.

LXXXII. HŎ-HPAI—FOREIGN TABLETS.

Hŏ-hpai, or " Foreign tablets," is the name given to the most popular Korean game of Dominoes, which is played by three or four persons. When four play the entire set of dominoes are used, but when three play the following pieces are withdrawn: $\frac{6}{6}$, $\frac{5}{5}$, $\frac{4}{4}$, and $\frac{3}{3}$.

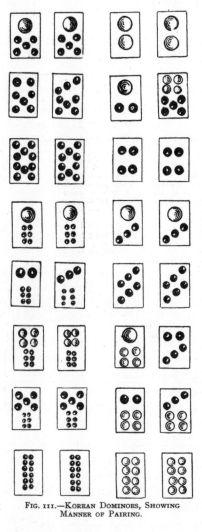

The dominoes are turned face down and shuffled. On commencing to play, all draw one piece to decide who shall play first. The one who gets the piece with the highest number of spots becomes the *Tjyang-ouen* (Chinese, *chong ün.*[1]) The pieces are again shuffled and the *Tjyang-ouen* draws seven pieces and each of the other players six. The *Tjyang-ouen* then whirls his seven pieces about between his fingers in his right hand until one of the pieces slips out. This piece he turns face up. Should the piece turned up be either $\frac{5}{4}$, $\frac{1}{2}$, $\frac{1}{4}$, or $\frac{2}{3}$, he keeps the pieces he has drawn. If it should be either $\frac{6}{6}$, $\frac{5}{5}$, $\frac{4}{4}$, $\frac{3}{3}$, $\frac{2}{2}$, $\frac{1}{1}$, $\frac{6}{4}$, $\frac{6}{1}$, $\frac{5}{1}$, or $\frac{3}{1}$—that is, one of the pieces of which there are duplicates—he hands his six pieces that are yet undiscovered to the player on his right, who in turn gives his pieces to his immediate neighbor, and so on in turn until the *Tjyang-ouen* receives those of the fourth player. If, on the other hand, he turns up either $\frac{6}{3}$, $\frac{6}{2}$, $\frac{5}{4}$, $\frac{5}{3}$, $\frac{4}{3}$, or $\frac{4}{2}$, he hands his six pieces to the player on his left, who in turn gives them to his immediate neighbor until the *Tjyang-ouen* receives those from the player on the right. The seventh piece that was turned up is now turned down and mixed with the remaining

FIG. 111.—KOREAN DOMINOES, SHOWING MANNER OF PAIRING.

---

[1] This title is that of the first of the Hanlin doctors in China. The same name is applied to the first of the literary graduates in Korea.

PLATE XXI.   KOREAN DOMINOES.

pieces, which are placed side by side in a line and covered with a slip of paper or with a strip of bamboo made for the purpose. If the *Tjyang-ouen* keeps his pieces he becomes the first player, but if he exchanges them, the one on the right or left, to whom he gave them, becomes the first player.

In this game certain combinations of three pieces are called *han-hpai*—(Chinese, *yat p'ái*)—"perfect tablets." The object of the game is for a player to get two such combinations. The game is then said to be *hte-tjye-ta*—"broken." *Hō-hpai* is played for money, and a certain stake is agreed upon, the player winning once, twice, thrice, four or five times this amount from each player, according to the particular combination which composes his winning hand. These combinations and the number they count are as follows:

1. A sequence, as $\frac{1}{3}$, $\frac{2}{4}$, $\frac{5}{6}$, called *ssang-syo-han-hpai* (Chinese, *shéung tsü yat p'ái*), counts three in combination with another *ssang-syo*, and one in combination with any other *han-hpai*. A *ssang-syo* composed of six pieces, which pair, according to the Korean system (Fig. 109), is called *tăi-să-ttai* (Chinese, *túi sz' tai*). "corresponding four times," and counts four, the name referring to the counts.

2. The sequence $\frac{1}{1}$, $\frac{1}{2}$, $\frac{1}{3}$, $\frac{1}{4}$, $\frac{1}{5}$, $\frac{1}{6}$, and the corresponding sequences in which 6, 5, 4, 3, and 2 replace the "ones" in the example given, are called *pou-tong* (Chinese, *pat t'ung*), "unlike," and count as follows:

1–1, 1–2, 1–3, 1–4, 1–5, 1–6, counts 3.
2–1, 2–2, 2–3, 2–4, 2–5, 2–6, counts 5.
3–1, 3–2, 3–3, 3–4, 3–5, 3–6, counts 3.
4–1, 4–2, 4–3, 4–4, 4–5, 4–6, counts 3.
5–1, 5–2, 5–3, 5–4, 5–5, 5–6, counts 4.
6–1, 6–2, 6–3, 6–4, 6–5, 6–6, counts 3.

3. The sequence $\frac{1}{2}$, $\frac{3}{6}$, $\frac{4}{5}$, $\frac{1}{4}$, $\frac{2}{6}$, $\frac{3}{5}$, called *hol-ssang-syo* (Chinese, *tuk shéung tsü*), "solitary double sequence," counts five.

4. Two doublets and one piece upon which the sum of the spots or one of the set of spots is equal to the single number of the doublets, as $\frac{5}{5}$, $\frac{5}{5}$, $\frac{1}{4}$, or $\frac{4}{4}$, $\frac{4}{4}$, $\frac{4}{2}$, called *sok* (Chinese, *noi*), "inclosed," counts one, both when paired with another *sok* or any other *han-hpai*. A *han-hpai* composed of sixes is called *ryouk-sok;* of fives, *o-sok;* of fours, *hong-sok;* of threes, *sam-sok;* of twos, *a-sok*, and of ones, *păik-sok*.

5. Three pieces upon which the spots are equally divided between two numbers, as $\frac{4}{4}$, $\frac{2}{4}$, $\frac{2}{2}$, called *tai săm tong* (Chinese, *túi săm t'ung*), "agreeing three alike," count one.

6. The combination $\frac{8}{8}$, $\frac{5}{5}$, $\frac{4}{4}$, called *ro-in* (Chinese, *lò yan*), " old man," counts three when combined with itself and one with any other *han-hpai*.

7. The combination $\frac{3}{3}$, $\frac{2}{2}$, $\frac{1}{1}$, called *a-ki* (Chinese, *á chi*), "child," counts three when combined with itself, and one with any other *han-hpai*.

8. The combination $\frac{6}{6}$, $\frac{3}{3}$, $\frac{2}{2}$, called *ssang-pyen* (Chinese, *shéung pin*), " doublets," counts three when combined with itself, and one with any other *han-hpai*.

9. The combinations $\frac{3}{3}$, $\frac{1}{1}$, $\frac{1}{2}$ and $\frac{4}{4}$, $\frac{5}{5}$, $\frac{6}{6}$, called *yo-soun*,[1] count three when combined with each other, and one with any other combination.

As the *sok* are the easiest combinations which may be formed, it is sometimes agreed to play without counting them.

If the first player has not drawn a winning hand, he puts down a piece from his hand at the end that is nearest to him of the concealed row, and takes up a piece at the other end, at the same time sliding the row of pieces along, so that the piece he puts down is concealed. If he does not then make a winning combination, the next player, if he has not already a winning hand, puts down a piece, and takes up another as before; and this is continued until some one obtains a winning combination and wins the game. He becomes the *Tjyang-ouen* in the next game.

LXXXIII. TJAK-MA-TCHO-KI—PAIR-MATING.

Tjak-ma-tcho-ki is played by two, three, or four persons. The pieces are reversed and shuffled and covered with paper. The first player draws six and the others each five dominoes. The first player endeavors to play out a pair from those he has drawn, but if he is unsuccessful he lays out one piece, face up, on the table. The second player takes up the discarded piece if he can combine it with a domino in his hand to form a pair. If not, he draws a piece from those left under the paper, and discards a domino which he lays out, face up. This process is repeated around until one player gets three pairs in his hand and wins the game. When two or three play the $\frac{6}{8}$ cannot be played to complete the third pair, but when four play it may be thus played, and the winner is paid only by the player who discarded the corresponding piece. If a pair is completed by a piece drawn from the unused pile, all the other players must pay the winner; but if it is completed with a piece which has been discarded, the player who discards that piece alone pays the winner. It is sometimes agreed that the third pair, by which a player wins, must be completed by a piece from the unused pile.

---

[1] *Yo-soun*, or Yao and Shun, the names of the two emperors who stand at the dawn of Chinese history as the models of all wisdom and sovereign virtue.—*Chinese Reader's Manual*, No. 900.

LXXXIV. KKO-RI-POUT-TCHI-KI—TAIL JOINING.

Kko-ri-pout-tchi-ki is played by two, three, or four persons. Three or four usually play. The set of dominoes is reversed and shuffled, and each player draws eight dominoes. When three play, the pieces $\frac{6}{8}$, $\frac{5}{5}$, $\frac{4}{4}$, and $\frac{2}{3}$ are first withdrawn. The game is opened by some one asking, Who has the *koan-i?* The holder of this piece, the $\frac{6}{2}$, lays down, face up, any piece he may choose from his hand, at the same time crying out one of the numbers on the sides of it, which number must be paired. The next player must mate the side designated with one of his pieces, failing in which he must lay a piece from his hand face down upon the table. The game is continued around until all have paired or laid down all their pieces. The players then count the spots on the pieces they have been compelled to lay down, which naturally have been selected from those with the fewest spots in their hands, and the one who has the highest number of spots pays the one who has the lowest number of spots. When four play, all players who count more than thirty must pay.

LXXXV. KOL-YE-SE—DOMINO YE-SE.

Kol-ye-se, that is, " Domino *Ye-se*," or the card game, *Ye-se*, with dominoes, is played by two or more persons, not exceeding ten. A set of dominoes is placed face down and shuffled, and part, if not all the pieces, are placed end to end in an irregular line. One of the players is designated as banker, *Moul-tjyou* (Chinese, *mat chü*), "things ruler." The other players each draw one piece in turn from the line. They examine this piece, and each puts down whatever stake they choose on the piece drawn. The *Moul-tjyou* puts down the same amount, whatever it may be, beside each player's stakes, and takes the next pieces. If his pieces are identical, a perfect pair, he at once wins all that has been staked. Otherwise the other players draw in turn either one or two pieces from the end of the line. This done, they and the *Moul-tjyou* turn their pieces face up. All count the spots on their dominoes. The remainders, after deducting the tens, count, and if the *Moul-tjyou* has an excess over the remainder of any player he takes his stakes, but if a player has an excess over that of the *Moul-tjyou* when the tens are deducted from the sum of the spots, the player wins the amount he has staked. This is a common game in gambling-houses. It is customary to keep a water-jar in such places, into which the players voluntarily put a portion of their stakes before the result is disclosed, or, if unmindful of the custom, at the suggestion of some one interested in the house.

LXXXVI. RYONG·HPAI—DRAGON TABLETS.

Dominoes are used in Korea in playing solitaire, which is a favorite kind of sortilege, not regarded seriously, but often played at the beginning of the day, the player wishing for a happy omen. One of the favorite games is called *Ryong-hpai* (Chinese, *lung p'ái*), "Dragon tablets."

One set of dominoes are placed face down and arranged in the form of a pyramid, with two pieces at the apex, and four, five, six, seven, and

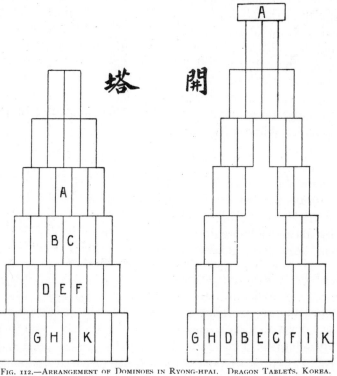

FIG. 112.—ARRANGEMENT OF DOMINOES IN RYONG-HPAI. DRAGON TABLETS. KOREA.

eight pieces in the successive rows beneath, as shown in the diagram on the left of Fig. 112. The centre domino, A, on the third row from the top, is then pushed down, taking with it the small pyramid composed of the pieces B C of the fourth row, D E F of the fifth row, and G H I K of the sixth row. The piece A is then placed transversely, face up, across the top of the original pyramid, and the other pieces that were withdrawn formed into a line, face up, at its base, the pairs G H and I K being put at the ends, D F within them, B C next within and E in the middle, as shown in the diagram on the right of Fig. 112. The player then proceeds to mate the pieces that are face up according to the Korean system, Fig. 111. When no more pairs can be made with the exposed pieces, the outside piece on the right of the second row from the top may be reversed. If it cannot be paired, it is left in its place; but if mated, the outside piece on the third row is liberated, and may be reversed, and so on. When the right-hand side is blocked, the piece on the left of the second row may be reversed, and the same plan followed as before.

When the piece A is mated, the two pieces beneath it may be reversed, and the removal of the two pieces at the ends of the lowest row, as G H, permits the piece directly above them to be reversed. The process is continued until the game is blocked or the player has mated all the pieces composing the pyramid. This game is known to the Cantonese laborers in the United States under the name of *Hoi t'áp,* "Opening the Pagoda," and is regarded by them as a means of divination.

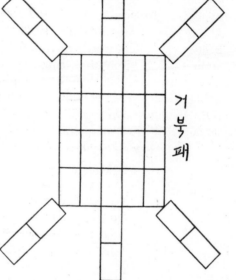

Fig. 113.—Arrangement of Dominoes in Ke-pouk-hpai. Tortoise Tablets. Korea.

LXXXVII. KE-POUK-HPAI[1]—TORTOISE TABLETS.

In this game the 32 dominoes are laid face down to form a representation of a tortoise, Fig. 113, with two pieces at the head and tail, and two for legs at each of the four corners. The pieces at these extremities are then turned face up and mated according to the Korean system, Fig. 111. The player loses if he fails to mate all the pieces.

LXXXVIII. SIN-SYO-TYEM.

Sin-syo-tyem (Chinese, *shan shò chim*), "Personally counting divination," is a kind of fortune-telling practiced in Korea with dominoes. The

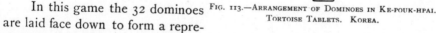

---

[1] Chinese, *kwai p'ái.*

inquirer shuffles a set of dominoes face down, and arranges them side by side in a line. He then turns them all face up, and selects as many of the combinations called *han-hpai*, referred to on pages 105, 106, as can be formed by contiguous pieces. The sum of the numbers there given in connection with each of the combinations thus formed is noted and the operation twice repeated. The three results are then added together, and if their sum amounts to 32, the number of the domino pieces, the augury is very good, more or less being estimated proportionally good or indifferent.

A somewhat similar method of fortune-telling with dominoes is current in China and practiced by the Chinese in the United States. The rules are given in a little hand-book entitled *Ngá p'ái shan shò t'ò chü ts'éung kái*, "Ivory domino divine number chart-commentary, completely explained." This work was printed in Canton in 1865, the name of the author being given as Ch'ing Ngok. The preface, which professes to explain the attributes and astrological significance of the dominoes, is followed by a series of diagrams illustrating different combinations formed with dominoes taken three, or in one class, two at a time. Specimens of the different classes are represented in Fig. 114.

The following names and numerical values are given to them :

> *Pat t'ung*, "unlike," counts 6.
> *Hòp háu*, "united ingenuity," counts 4.
> *'Ng tsz'*, "five spots," counts 5.
> *Fan séung*, "divided appearance," counts 3.
> *Má kwan*, "cavalry," counts 3.
> *I sám luk*, "two, three, six," counts 3.
> *Iú i sám*, "ace, two, three," counts 3.
> *Túi tsz'*, "corresponding spots," counts 3.
> *Ching fái*, "very easy," counts 1.

In telling fortunes an entire set of dominoes is placed face down upon a table and well mixed. The dominoes are then all placed side by side in a row and reversed. The manipulator selects from this row as many combinations as possible, formed by adjacent pieces, according to the diagrams, and adds together the numbers corresponding with them. This sum is referred to the following table and the result noted:

> 1 to 4 is to be esteemed *há há*, "lowest."
> 5 to 7 is to be esteemed *chung há*, "below the middle."
> 8 to 9 is to be esteemed *chung p'ing*, "even middle."
> 10 to 11 is to be esteemed *shéung shéung*, "highest."

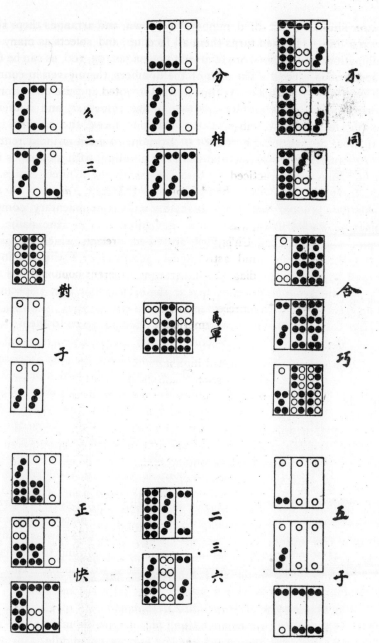

FIG. 114.—COMBINATIONS OF DOMINOES, SIGNIFICANT IN FORTUNE-TELLING. CHINA.

The dominoes are then reversed again and mixed, and the preceding operations twice repeated and three sets of terms from the above series obtained. Reference is then made to the text of the book. This consists of 125 pages, arranged in order under all the different combinations that may be formed with the five pairs of terms given above, taken three pairs at a time, commencing with *shéung shéung, shéung shéung, shéung shéung.* An oracular verse, apparently of original composition, is found on each page, referring to some well-known personage or incident, with a short text to aid the diviner in applying the prognostication to the various affairs of life.

LXXXIX. O-KOAN—FIVE GATEWAYS.

Another popular method of divination with dominoes is called *O-koan* (Chinese, *'ng kwán*), "Five gateways." An entire set of dominoes is reversed and shuffled, and twenty pieces are then arranged in five rows of four pieces each, Fig. 115.

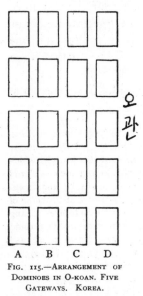

The player turns these pieces face up, and, commencing at the bottom row, endeavors to form combinations of three pieces each, *han-hpai*, such as have been described under *Hō-hpai* (LXXXII). In addition to the *han-hpai* already enumerated, pp. 105, 106, the following additional ones are permitted in *O-koan:* three pieces upon which three of the spots are alike, and the sum of the other three sets of spots is equal to five, called *sam-tong-tan-o-tyem* (Chinese, *sám t'ung tán 'ng tím*), "three alike and only five spots;" and three pieces upon which three of the spots are alike, and the sum of the other three sets of spots is equal to or more than fourteen, called *sam-tong-sip-să-tyem* (Chinese, *sám t'ung shap sz' tím*), "three alike and fourteen spots."

A   B   C   D

FIG. 115.—ARRANGEMENT OF DOMINOES IN O-KOAN. FIVE GATEWAYS. KOREA.

In forming these combinations, three contiguous pieces in a row may be taken, or one or two pieces at one end of a row may be used in combination with two pieces or one piece at the other end, the pieces thus taken being always placed on the inner side. Thus, the piece A, Fig. 115, may be mated with C D to form a combination A C D, or A B may be mated with D to form a combination A B D. The combinations thus formed are removed and placed in a row, face up, above the five rows, the one formed nearest the bottom being placed to the left and successive ones to the right of the line thus created. When no more combinations can be discovered, five pieces are drawn from the unused pile of twelve pieces, which have been left with their faces down, and one of them placed face down to the right of each of the five rows. These five pieces are then turned face up, and an attempt made to form combinations of threes with their aid. The results are successively placed to the right of the line at the top, and this process is continued until the twelve extra pieces are exhausted. When this happens, five pieces are withdrawn from the left of the top line, and added in succession to the right of the five rows. If by chance but four or a less number of rows remain, only a corresponding number of pieces are drawn. This process is continued over and over until all the pieces are combined in sets of threes in a long row at the top, or the top row is exhausted and a block ensues, determining success or failure in the game.

The name of the game is said to have been taken from a well-known episode in the life of Koan Ou (Chinese, *Kwán Ü*[1]), the celebrated Chinese general, now universally worshiped in China as the God of War, and one of the famous heroes of the Chinese romance, the *Sám Kwok Chí*, or "Annals of the Three States."[2]

In escaping from Ts'ao Ts'ao,[3] it is recorded he killed six generals at

---

[1] Wylie's *Notes on Chinese Literature*, p. 161.

[2] Kwan Yü (*Kwán Ü*) D. A. D. 219. Designated Kwan Chwang Miú, and deified as Kwan Ti or Wú Ti, the god of war. A native of Kiai Chow in Shan-si, who rose to celebrity toward the close of the second century through his alliance with Liu Pei and Chang Fei in the struggles which ushered in the period of the Three Kingdoms. He is reputed in early life to have been a seller of bean-curd, but to have subsequently applied himself to study, until, in A. D. 184, he casually encountered Liu Pei at a time when the latter was about to take up arms in defense of the house of Han against the rebellion of the Yellow Turbans. He joined Liu Pei and his confederate, Chang Fei, in a solemn oath, which was sworn in a peach orchard belonging to the latter, that they would fight thenceforth side by side and live and die together. The fidelity of Kwan Yü to his adopted leader remained unshaken during a long series of years in despite of many trials, and similarly his attachment to Chang Fei continued throughout their lives. At an early period of his career he was created a t'ing how (baron) by the regent Ts'ao Ts'ao, with the title of Hán Shau t'ing hau. . . . His martial prowess shone conspicuously in many campaigns which were waged by Lui Pei before his throne as sovereign of Shuh became assured; but he fell a victim at last to the superior force and strategy of Sun K'üan, who took him prisoner and caused him to be beheaded. Long celebrated as one of the most renowned among Chinese heroes, he was at length canonized by the superstitious Hwei Tsung, of the Sung dynasty, early in the twelfth century, with the title of Chung Hwui Kung. In 1128 he received the still higher title of Chwáng Miú Wú Ngán Wang, and after many subsequent alterations and additions he was at length raised, in 1594, by Ming Wan Li to the rank of Ti or god, since which date, and especially since the accession of the Manchow dynasty, his worship as the God of War has been firmly established.—*Chinese Reader's Manual*, No. 297.

[3] Ts'ao Ts'ao, D. A. D. 220.—*Chinese Reader's Manual*, No. 768.

" five frontier passes," *o-koan* (Chinese, *'ng kwán*). The vicissitudes of his life at this time are typified in the varying fortunes of the game, which at one moment approaches a successful termination, only for the player to be set back unexpectedly to overcome its obstacles anew. The conquest of the five *kwán* which *Kwán Ü* achieved finds an analogue in the five rows of dominoes which the player struggles to overcome. Many educated people in Korea play this game every morning, and scholars who have nothing to do play it all the day long, finding intellectual pastime in its elusive permutations.

The game of Dominoes is not commonly known in Japan, except as introduced as a foreign game from Europe, but I am informed by Mr. Julius Matsumoto that a native game is played secretly by gamblers in Central Japan, being called *Ten sho* (Chinese, *t'in shü*), " Heavenly writings." He describes the dominoes as colored, decorated with silver and gold. They probably agree with the domino cards which are common in different parts of China.

Dominoes are the most popular game in China at the present day. They are made of wood, ivory, and bone in a variety of forms, and are commonly known as *Kwat p'ái*, or " Bone tablets," as in Korea. A set consists of thirty-two pieces, marked in the same manner as those of Korea, but they are paired differently, as shown in Fig. 116, and are ordinarily divided into two suits or series called *man*, " civil," and *mò*, " military," which receive the following names :

Man, or " civil."

> 6–6, called *t'in*, " Heaven."
> 1–1, called *tí*, " Earth."
> 4–4, called *yan*, " Man."
> 1–3, called *wo*, " Harmony."
> 5–5, called *múi*, " plum flower."
> 5–3, called *chéung sám*, " long threes."
> 2–2, called *pán tang*, " bench."
> 6–5, called *fú t'au*, " tiger's head."
> 6–4, called *hung t'au shap*, " red-head ten."
> 6–1, called *kò kéuk ts'at*, " long-leg seven."
> 5–1, called *hung ch'ui luk*, " red-mallet six."

There are two pieces of each of the above, which mate with each other, in a set.

Mò, or "military."

2–4 and 1–2, called *chí tsün*, "supreme."

6–3 and 4–5, called *tsáp kau*, "heterogenous nines."

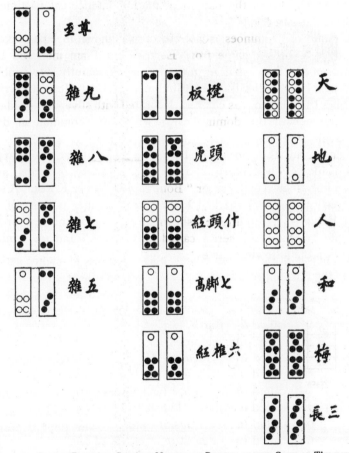

武子   文子

至尊

雜九   板櫈   天

雜八   虎頭   地

雜七   紅頭什   人

雜五   高脚七   和

       紅椎六   梅

                 長三

FIG. 116.—CHINESE DOMINOES, SHOWING MANNER OF PAIRING IN THE GAME OF T'IN KAU OR "HEAVENS AND NINES."

6–2 and 5–3, called *tsáp pát*, "heterogenous eights."

4–3 and 5–2, called *tsáp ts'at*, "heterogenous sevens."

1–4 and 2–3, called *tsáp 'ng*, "heterogenous fives."

8

116

The two pieces called *chi tsün*, or " supreme," are together the highest of the " military " series, but separately, rank as the lowest.

The dominoes in common use in the Province of Kwangtung and among the Chinese in the United States are made of Chinese ebony, and are about two and five-eighths inches long, seven-eighths of an inch in width, and

FIG. 117.—KWAT P'ÁI. DOMINOES. KWANGTUNG, CHINA.

three-eighths of an inch in thickness, with incised spots, which are painted red and white. The ends of each piece are usually ornamented with a single incised red spot, while the backs are sometimes uniformly marked with three spots, one red between two white, arranged diagonally across, Fig. 117. Small dominoes of bone, or bone and wood conjoined, of the same size as those of Korea, are used at Fuhchau and Shanghai and other parts of China.[1]

The Chinese in the United States play a number of games with dominoes. At the opening of games, the pieces are usually piled in the manner shown in Fig. 118, called *shéung tung*, or " stack."

TIÚ Ü.

A simple Chinese game called *Tiú ü*, " To angle," is played by two or three persons, with two sets of dominoes. The pieces are well mixed and piled face down, side by side, in a stack four high. Four piles of four each

FIG. 118.—STACK OF DOMINOES AT OPENING OF GAMES.

---

[1] A set from Canton (No. 41) in Mr. Wilkinson's collection, in the University Museum, is made of bone with bamboo backs, and another set (No. 40) in the same collection, from Shanghai, is of bone with black wood backs. A set from Fuhchau, in the University Museum, is made entirely of bamboo, with slightly curved faces that follow the natural curve of the reed. The spots are painted red and green, green taking the place of the black spots.

are now drawn from one end of the stack and placed face up on the table. When two play, both players draw three piles (twelve dominoes), or if three play, two piles (eight dominoes) from the same end of the bank. The players then examine their pieces, and the first player endeavors to mate one of his pieces with one having the same number of spots among those turned up on the table. If successful, he places the mated pair, face up, before him. In either case he draws the bottom piece of the pile at the end of the stack from which the last piles were drawn and endeavors to mate it with one of those on the table. If successful, he takes the pair, but if not, he places the piece drawn among those on the table. The second player then tries to mate one of his pieces, and also draws one from the stack, and the game is continued in this manner until the stack is exhausted. A pair of double "sixes" in a player's hand is at once laid out. If a player holds a piece in his hand, identical with two pieces on the table, and the fourth piece of the same kind has not been played, he may, at his turn, pile the three pieces that are alike one upon the other, with the uppermost face up, at the opposite end of the stack to that drawn from, and the player who first lays out the fourth piece may take the three pieces. The two pieces composing the *chí tsün* mate with each other, and form an exception in this game to the rule by which all pieces having the same number of spots mate with each other without reference to their belonging either to the *man* or *mò* series. When the last domino is drawn, the players examine those they have taken. The pieces on which the spots number eight or more are called *tái ü*, "large fish," and count two points for each spot. The pieces below eight are called *sai ü*, "small fish," and count one point for each red spot. If this latter sum is between two decades, the highest decade is counted. The player counting the highest becomes the winner, and is paid by each of the players for each point he has in excess.

TSUNG SHAP.

Tsung shap, "To dispute for tens," is played by two persons with one set of dominoes. The pieces are piled face down, side by side, in a stack four pieces high, which the players divide between them, each player taking eight of the sixteen piles. The first player draws the top piece from the end pile toward the right of his pile, and lays it face up on the table. The second player, in turn, draws a piece and lays it face up alongside of the piece played by the first player. The players continue to draw and place the pieces on the table in this manner either on the right or left of the row thus formed. If a player lays down a piece which is a duplicate of one of the pieces at either end of the row, he takes both pieces, called *túi*, a " pair," and they count ten for each spot on them at the end of the game. Or, if a player lays down a piece on which the spots, added to those on two pieces at one end of the row, or on the pieces at each end, form a sum that is a multiple of ten, the player takes the three pieces, and they count one for each spot on them at the end of the game. If there are but two pieces on the table, and a player takes them, he piles them upon each other to mark the play, called *táp tí*—*i. e.*, a " sweep," which counts forty. The winner draws and lays out another piece. Should he fail to take up a winning combination of two or three pieces his opponent may take it, and follow by laying out a piece and continuing the game. The game proceeds until one of the players has laid out all of his pieces, when the one who counts highest wins.

K'AP T'ÁI SHAP.

K'im t'ái shap, " To grasp many tens ;" *Ch'i t'ái shap*, " To grasp many tens," or *K'ap t'ái shap*, " To complete many tens," is played by any number of persons from two to twenty and upward, and is the favorite game with dominoes in the Chinese gambling-houses in the United States. In many of these houses a large table covered with matting to deaden the sound is kept apart for this game. As there played, many sets of dominoes are used, which are well mixed by the players and piled faces down, side by side, in piles five pieces high in a long stack upon the table. The croupier, or one of the players, shakes four dice under a cup, and counts around to the right, commencing with the player on his right, up to the number thrown. The one at whom he stops becomes the first player. The top piece on the third pile from one end of the stack, with each alternate piece on the top up to the number of persons playing, less one, is now removed and placed in a pile at the other end of the stack. The first player takes two piles at the end and gets ten pieces, the second player on his right takes the two next piles and gets nine pieces, and so on, each player except the first getting nine pieces.

In this game, each piece in a set of dominoes may be mated with a duplicate piece to form a pair called *ngán*, " eye." The *ngán* or eyes thus formed by the pieces on the left, Fig. 119, are called *ün ngán* or " weak eyes," while those formed by the pieces on the right are called *ngáng ngán*, or " strong eyes." The object of the game is to get ten pieces in each of which two are the same, and form either an *ün* or *ngáng ngán*, and the others form four pairs, in each of which the sum of the spots is ten or a multiple of ten, whence the name of the game. The piece 2–4 is only counted as three in making up tens.

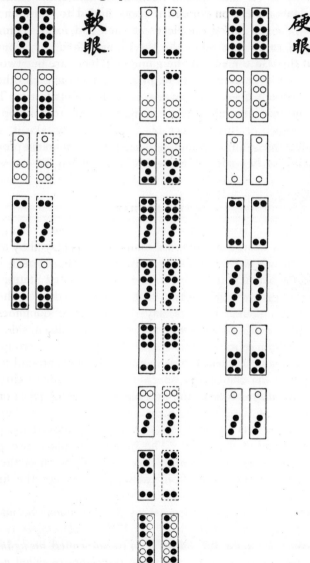

FIG. 119.—METHOD OF PAIRING CHINESE DOMINOES IN THE GAME OF K'AP T'ÁI SHAP.

The players examine their pieces, and the first player, if he has not drawn a winning hand, discards a piece, which he throws face up on the table. The next player to the right may take this piece to complete a winning hand, or in exchange for a piece from his hand, which he places face up on the table. He also draws a piece from the bottom of the exposed pile of the stack. If it does not complete a winning hand 'he may either throw it face up on the table or keep it and discard a piece from his hand. The third player may now take one of the pieces on the table and draw one from the bottom of the exposed pile. The game proceeds in this way until one of the players gets ten pieces, of which two form a *ngán*, and the others pairs on which the sum of the spots is ten or a multiple of ten, and wins the game.

In gambling-houses the stakes are placed in a box on the table at the commencement of each game, the players all contributing the same amount. Five per cent. is at once taken from the box for the gambling-house, and the remainder goes to the successful player.

K'AP SHAP.

K'ap shap, " To complete tens ;" *K'im shap,* " To grasp tens ;" *Shap tsai,* " Little tens." *K'ap shap* corresponds with the preceding game, and is the name given to it when played by two persons. One set of dominoes are used, and the pieces are arranged in a stack four high. The first player takes eight and the second seven pieces. The object of the game is to get eight pieces, two of which form a *ngán*, or pair, and the others pairs on which the sum of the spots is ten or a multiple of ten. In this game, as in *K'ap t'ái shap*, a winning hand is required to contain one *ngán*, or " eye." Slight variations from the manner here described occur in playing these games. The first player is frequently determined by drawing a domino and counting around, instead of by throwing dice.

NAU T'IN KAU.

Nau t'in kau, literally " Turning Heavens and Nines," from the names of the highest pieces of the two suits, is played by two persons. One set of dominoes are used, which are piled face down in a stack four high. The first player draws the top domino from the end of the stack toward his right, and the second player the one beneath it. The second player must draw a higher domino of the same suit, either *man* or *mò*, or the first player takes both pieces and places them on the table before him, with the face of the winning piece exposed on top. The winner continues drawing first until the other player draws a higher piece, when the latter takes both pieces and has the lead. The game is continued in this way until the stack is exhausted.

Each of the players then counts the red spots on the exposed faces of the dominoes before him, and the one having the highest total becomes the winner, and is paid for each red spot he has in excess by the loser.

TÁ T'IN KAU.

Tá t'in kau, "To play Heavens and Nines," called, like the preceding game, from the names of the highest pieces of the two suits, is the best and most interesting of the Chinese games with dominoes. It is played by four persons with one set of dominoes. The thirty-two pieces are arranged face down in a stack four high to form eight piles of four pieces each. One of the players throws two dice, and counts around to determine who shall be the first player. He is called *Tsò chong,* or *Chong ká,* and usually places some object on the table before him to indicate his position. A disk of wood, inscribed with the character *chong,* frequently accompanies sets of dominoes for this purpose. The first player takes two piles of dominoes. If the dice fall near one end of the stack of dominoes, the first player takes the two piles at that end, the player on his right the next two piles, the third player to the right the next two, and the fourth player the remaining rows. But if the dice fall near the middle of the stack, the first player takes the two middle rows, the player on his right the piles on the right and left of the middle ones, the third player the piles outside of these, and the fourth player the piles at the ends. The first player leads by placing one, two, three, or four pieces face up on the table. One piece of either suit may be thus led, and a higher piece of the same suit will be required to take it; or a pair of either suit may be led, and a higher pair of the same suit will be required to take it; or one or both pieces of the first, second, third, or fourth pair of one suit (see Fig. 119) may be led with one or both pieces of the corresponding pair of the other suit, and two, three, or four pieces of corresponding higher pairs will be required to take them; that is, one or both of the $\frac{6}{6}$ may be led with one or both of the pair $\frac{6}{3}$, $\frac{4}{4}$, and the pair of $\frac{1}{1}$ with one or both of the pair $\frac{6}{2}$, $\frac{5}{5}$, and *vice versa.*

The other players follow from right to left by playing as many pieces as are led, putting them on top of those on the table if they are higher, or beneath if they are lower than those already played. They are not required to follow suit. The winner leads again, and the game is continued until all the dominoes have been played. The player who takes the last round wins the game. He becomes the *Tsò chong* for the next game. It is required of the winner, however, to take at least two tricks, so that if only one piece is led on the last round a player who has not won a trick is not allowed to take the trick, and the game goes to the next higher player. *Tá t'in kau* is invariably played for money. A trick counts one point, for which any sum may be agreed upon. At the end of the game the players each pay the winner according to the number of tricks they have taken. The holder of four or more tricks pays nothing; of two tricks, for two points; of one trick, for three points, and a player who does not take a trick, for five points. The first player, or *Tsò chong*, however, always pays twice the amount when he loses and is paid double when he wins, and so on throughout the game, paying and receiving in every case twice as much as the other players. Should the *Tsò chong*, through winning the last round, hold his position over into the next game, his gains and losses are then in the ratio of three to one to those of the other players. In the third game they would be as four to one, and so on.

If any player except the first player wins a round with the pair $\frac{2}{4}$, $\frac{1}{2}$, called *chi tsün*, the first player must pay him four times, and the other players twice the sum agreed upon for one point; but if the first player takes a round with the *chi tsün*, the other players must pay him four times the value of a point.

If any player except the first takes a round with four pieces of two corresponding pairs, the first player pays him eight times and the other players four times the value of a point, but if the first player takes the round the other players pay him eight times the value of a point. .

If a player takes two rounds with the *chi tsün* or two rounds with two corresponding pairs in two successive games, the amounts that must be paid him by the other players are doubled, and if he takes three such rounds in succession they are trebled. In gambling-houses the winner of a round with the *chi tsün* must put the value of one point and the winner with two corresponding pairs of two points in a box for the house. This constitutes the only revenue derived by gambling-houses from the game.

It is said that the custom of requiring the winner to take at least two tricks is an innovation of the last hundred years. Formerly the person taking the last trick became the winner, although it was the only trick taken by him during the game.

A comparison of the domino games of Korea with those of China shows that they are practically the same. The popular Korean game, called *Hö-hpai*, has many points of agreement with the Chinese method of telling fortunes with dominoes, and, in the opinion of the writer, dominoes originated in a divinatory system in which two dice were employed. The date of the invention of the implements is unknown.

It is recorded that their present form was fixed by an imperial edict in the time of Kao-tsung (1127–1163 A. D). A discussion of the origin of dominoes, with an account of the Burmese and Siamese games, will be found in the author's paper on *Chinese Games With Dice and Dominoes*. [1]

XC. HTOU-TJYEN.—PLAYING-CARDS.

Korean playing-cards consist of long narrow strips of oiled paper bearing upon their face highly-conventionalized written characters, which indicate their value. A pack of Korean cards (*a*) in the United States National Museum, Washington, consists of eighty marked cards and one blank, the latter probably used to supply a lost card. The backs are uniformly marked with the design represented in Fig. 120. There are eight suits of ten cards each, as follows:

> *Sa răm* (Chinese, *yan*), "man."
> *Moul-ko-ki* (Chinese, *ü*), "fish."
> *Ka-ma-koui* (Chinese, *ú*), "crow."
> *Kkoueng* (Chinese, *chí*), "pheasant."
> *No-ro* (Chinese, *chéung*), "antelope."
> *Pyel* (Chinese, *sing*), "star."
> *Htok-ki* (Chinese, *t'ó*), "rabbit."
> *Măl* (Chinese, *má*), "horse."

The cards of each suit are distinguished by numerals from one to nine for each suit, the tenth card being designated as *Tjyang* (Chinese, *tséung*), "General," Fig. 121. The numerals, Fig. 122, are placed above the suit-marks, Fig. 123. The name of the card is written in Chinese characters near the bottom of the "General" cards of this pack. Their dimensions are eight by one-fourth inches.

Another pack of Korean cards (*b*) in the Museum of Archæology of the University of Pennsylvania is similar to the preceding, except that it consists of sixty cards of six suits instead of eight, as follows: Man, Fish, Pheasant, Antelope, Rabbit, and Horse. There are two blank cards. The marks on the "General" cards are the same as those on the preceding pack, but the

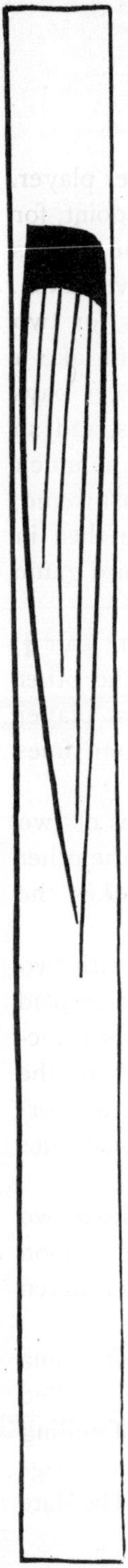

---

[1] Report of the United States National Museum for 1893.

Fig. 120.—Reverse of Korean Playing-Card.—Pack *c*.

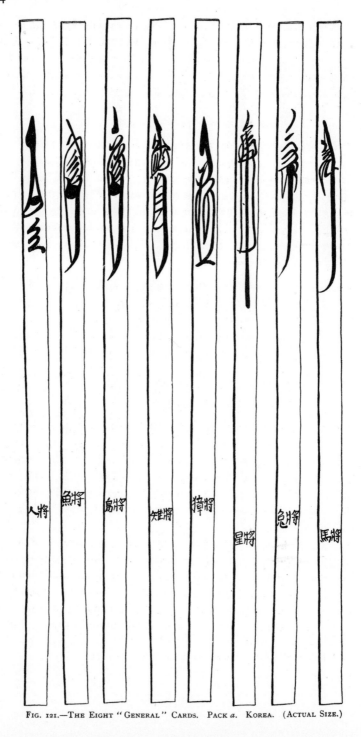

人將　魚將　鳥將　雉將　獐將　星將　兎將　馬將

FIG. 121.—THE EIGHT "GENERAL" CARDS. PACK *a*. KOREA. (ACTUAL SIZE.)

suit-marks on the numeral cards are even more conventionally written. There are no marks at the bottom of the "General" cards. Their dimen-

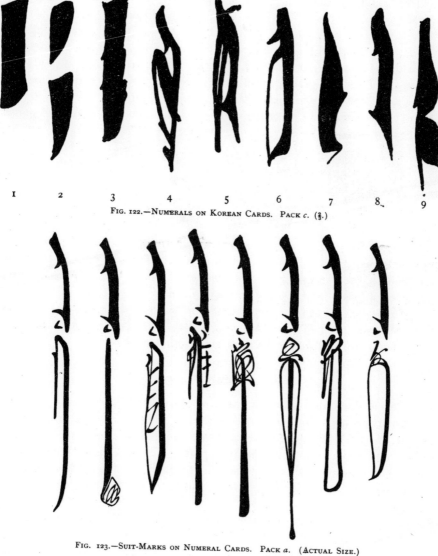

FIG. 122.—NUMERALS ON KOREAN CARDS. PACK *c.* (⅔.)

FIG. 123.—SUIT-MARKS ON NUMERAL CARDS. PACK *a.* (ACTUAL SIZE.)

sions are seven and five-eighths by one-half inches. The backs are decorated like the preceding.

Another pack of Korean cards (c) in the United States National Museum is identical with the preceding, except that the suit-marks are not distinguished on the numeral cards, all of them being marked alike with a character like that on the "Man" suit of the preceding pack.

It will be observed that the eight suit-marks of the Korean cards—Man, Fish, Crow, Pheasant, Antelope, Star, Rabbit, and Horse—are analogous to the *Pát Mat*, or "Eight Creatures," which correspond with the *Pát Kwá*, or "Eight Diagrams," namely: Horse, Ox, Dragon, Swine, Pheasant, Dog, and Goat (*má, ngau, lung, kai, ch'i, chí, kau, yéung*).

The *Dictionnaire Coréen-Français* gives the following names of games with cards:

Ka-keui (Chinese, *ká k'í*), "false or feigned chess."
Kop-soi, a synonym for *Htou-tjyen*.
Mok-tji (Chinese, *muk chí*), "eye paper."
Nek-tjyang-ke-ri (Chinese, *sz' chéung*), "four pages."
Sa-si-rang-i (Chinese, *hò siú ts'in*, "small cash").

None of the above names were familiar to my informants. Cards are the game of the lowest classes of men in Korea, and it is difficult to obtain information about them from educated men, although they are played for purposes of gambling by people of higher rank.

There are said to be a great number of games with cards. One of the principal ones is called *Htou-tjyen*. It is played by four persons who each take twenty cards, dividing the pack among them.

XCI. YET-PANG-MANG-I.[1]

This is a common game of cards in Korea, and corresponds with the Korean game with dominoes *Kol-ye-se* (No. LXXXV), which is said to have originated from this game. The cards are shuffled, as is customary, by the dealer, who divides the pack into two parts. These he holds at the top in each hand, drawing the ends of the cards, which lay side by side, through each other. Or, the cards are drawn out near the bottom and put upon the top.

One pack is used in this game, and any number may play. The game-

---

[1] *Yet-pang-mang-i* (*yet* is a "sweetmeat," *pang-mang-i* a "pestle" or "club") is the most popular game. Sometimes the same player holds the bank for three rounds, sometimes for five. The game is a favorite with the Korean sharper, who will abstract an extra card, or, if dealer, will place a *tjyang* and a *kou* (nine) where they will fall to himself.—WILKINSON.

양모노호쳔투

PLATE XXII.   KOREAN CARD PLAYING.

keeper, *Moul-tjyou* (see p. 107), deals a card face down to each player, including himself, always drawing the cards from the bottom instead of from the top. The players have all put down their wagers, which have been covered by corresponding amounts by the *Moul-tjyou*. The object of the game is to get two or three cards upon which the sum of the numerals is nine, called *kap-o*,[1] or nineteen, the tens not counting, and only the unit being significant. In default of achieving nine, the lower units count, eight being considered good. Each player then draws one or two cards from the bottom of the pack.

If the *Moul-tjyou* has an excess over any player, taking the sum of the numerals on his two or three cards, less the tens, he wins that player's stakes; but the players who count higher than the *Moul-tjyou*, each win an amount equal to their stakes from him. When both count alike, neither wins. Three cards having the same number count higher than nine. It will be observed that in this game the suit marks do not appear to be regarded, and it is to be inferred that the last-described pack (*c*), was especially intended for it.

Mr. Wilkinson placed in my hands the manuscript of his paper on Korean cards, to be published in the *Korean Repository*, from which I obtained the following additional particulars: As far as can be learned but one kind of *Htou-tjyen* is used, or ever has been used in Korea. The only distinction now observed is in the minor detail of the color of the backs, which in Hpyeng-an province are blackened completely instead of, as elsewhere, being marked with a harp-shaped scrawl. Four, six, and, until recent years, eight suits occur in a pack (*tjil*).[2] The Koreans themselves give the names of the suits differently. The usual list which he gives agrees with that furnished by my Korean informants.

"It is said that the early *Tjyang* ('General' cards) were pictures, more or less carefully drawn, of the various emblems portrayed, and the present scrawls are declared to be corruptions of these pictures. While the Koreans retain a tradition of the names of these emblems, they are not all agreed as to their significance. An explanation of this provoking vagueness is to be found in the circumstance that whereas in the ancient game of eighty cards it was necessary to carefully distinguish the *Tjyang*, in all modern games they are absolutely of equal value—are regarded, indeed, as tens."

---

[1] The *Dictionnaire Coréen-Français* defines *kap-o* as a "game of chance."

[2] Chinese, *tit*, meaning in China a cloth or paper case to cover Chinese books, and in Korea, "all the volumes of the same work."—*D. C. F.*

XCII. TONG-TANG.

"Another common game is *Tong-tang* (Chinese *t'ung tong*). When three or four players engage in it, the pack of forty is used; when five or six, the older pack of sixty. To decide who is to be leader, a single card is drawn by each player, the highest card winning. The leader receives six cards, the other players five apiece, dealt one at a time. The remainder, or stock, is either (1) held by one of the players, or (2) placed on the table, the cards radiating like the spokes of a wheel—except that one spoke in this case is imposed on the next, and that upon a third, and so on. The game proceeds as in the majority of Chinese card games, of which 'Khanhoo' lately introduced in England, may be taken as a type."

The Korean name of their cards, *Htou-tjyen*, is, according to the *Dictionnaire Coréen-Français*, the Chinese *tau tsin*. *Tau* means "to fight," and *tsin* (written with the radical *kwo*, a "spear," doubled, with *p'in*, "a splinter," on the left), "tablets or slips used to write on." The name, then, might be translated as "fighting tablets." The heart-shaped scroll on the back of the cards, Fig. 120, however, reveals their true significance. This mark is a survival of one of the feathers of the arrow from which they were derived. Mr. Cushing has suggested to me that the numerals, Fig. 122, are also derived from feathers, being survivals of the cut cock-feathers of the original arrows. The suit-marks may be regarded as the totemic animals of the Eight Directions, and, as before mentioned, agree somewhat closely, although evidently earlier, with the Eight Creatures that correspond with the Eight Diagrams. As to the form of the cards, they are clearly copied from slips of bamboo, such as are used as divining lots at the present day in China. In fact, an almost exact replica of the Korean pack is to be found in the eighty consecutively numbered lots, *ts'im,* used by Chinese gamblers to divine the lucky numbers in the lottery called *Pák kòp piú.*[1] The latter retain the arrow-like tip, while the cards bear the arrow feathers, and the names of both are almost identical with that of arrow, *tsin.*

From the preceding it will appear that *Htou-tjyen* is a game of "fighting arrows." The relations of the *Htou-tjyen* to other playing-cards is discussed at the close of the account of Chinese playing-cards in the following pages.

Playing-cards are known in Japan as *karuta,* a word derived from the

---

[1] The numbered lots, *mikuji,* used in Japanese temples, which correspond with the Chinese *ts'im ü,* agree exactly in size and form with the Korean cards.

Portuguese *carta*. They also receive the name of *fuda* (Chinese, *chát*, a "bundle"), or *bakuchi no fuda*, that is, "gambling cards."[1] There are several kinds in general use, of which the commonest, which are used for gambling,[2] are called *Hana-garuta*, or "Flower cards," and the game which is played with them, *Hana-awase*, or "Flower matching." *Hana-garuta* are made of cardboard, and are usually about one and three-quarters by one and one-eighth inches. The backs are black and the faces bear pictures in colors. A pack comprises forty-eight cards divided into twelve sets, or suits, of four cards each. The suit-marks are flowers and other emblems appropriate to the twelve months of the year. The cards in each suit vary in value from one to twenty points, called *ten* (Chinese, *tim*, "spot"). One or two cards in each suit bear only the emblem of the suit and count one point. With two exceptions there is one card in each suit that has in addition the picture of a *Tanzaku*, "a kind of paper or thin wood used for writing verses on." These count five. The other cards bear other emblems in addition to that of the suit, and count 10 and 20. The suit-marks and their several cards are as follows :

1. *Matsu*, "Pine," corresponds to first month :
   Two *Matsu* (plain), each count one point.
   Tanzaku matsu counts 5.
   Matsu ni tsuru, "Pine and Stork," counts 20.
2. *Ume*, "Plum," corresponds to second month :
   Two *Ume* (plain), each count 1.
   Tanzaku ume counts 5.
   Ume ni uguisu, "Plum and Singing Bird,"[3] counts 10.
3. *Sakura*, "Cherry," corresponds to third month :
   Two *Sakura* (plain), each count 1.
   Tanzaku sakura counts 5.
   Sakura ni maku, "Cherry and Curtain," counts 20.
4. *Fugi*, "Wisteria," corresponds to fourth month :
   Two *Fugi* (plain), each count 1.
   Tanzaku fugi counts 5.
   Fugi ni hototogisu, "Wisteria and Cuckoo," counts 10.

---

[1] Hepburn's *Dictionary* gives *kwat p'ái*, or "dominoes," as the Chinese equivalent for *karuta*.

[2] Gamblers in Japan usually play with *Hana-garuta*, or with dice. They are said to unite in secret societies, which are suppressed by the government. A piece of stone from the tombstone of a famous gambler is regarded by them as bringing luck and is carried as a charm.

[3] *Cettria cantans*, Hepburn's *Dictionary*.

5. *Ayame*, "Sweet Flag," corresponds to fifth month :
   Two *Ayame* (plain), each count 1.
   Tanzaku ayame counts 5.
   Ayame ni hotaru, "Sweet Flag and Fire-fly," counts 10.

6. *Botan*, "Peony," corresponds to sixth month :
   Two *Botan* (plain), each count 1.
   Tanzaku botan counts 5. This card is called *Awotan*, or "blue *Tanzaku*," from the *Tanzaku* being blue. On the others, with two exceptions, it is red.
   Botan ni cho, "Peony and Butterfly," counts 10.

7. *Hagi*, "Lespedeza," or "Bush Clover," corresponds to seventh month :
   Two *Hagi* (plain), each count 1.
   Tanzaku hagi counts 5.
   Hagi ni inoshishi, "Peony and Wild Boar," counts 10.

8. *Susuki*, "Eularia," corresponds with eighth month :
   Two *Susuki* (plain), each count 1.
   Susuki ni karigane, "Eularia and Wild Goose," counts 10.
   Susuki ni tsuki, "Eularia and Moon," counts 20.

9. *Kiku*, "Chrysanthemum," corresponds to ninth month :
   Two *Kiku* (plain), each count 1.
   Tanzaku kiku (blue) counts 5.
   Kiku ni sakazuki, "Chrysanthemum and Wine Cup," counts 10.

10. *Momiji*, "Maple," corresponds to tenth month :
    Two *Momiji* (plain), each count 1.
    Tanzaku momiji (blue) counts 5.
    Momiji ni shika, "Maple and Deer," count 10.

11. *Ame*, "Rain," corresponds to the eleventh month :
    One *Ame* (plain), counts 1.
    Tanzaku ame counts 5.
    Ame ni tsubame, "Rain and Swallow," counts 10.
    Ame ni yanagi, "Rain and Willow," counts 20. The last card bears a picture of a frog and a man, referring to a story.

12. *Kiri*, "Paullownia," corresponds to twelfth month :
    Three *Kiri* (plain), each count 1.
    Kiri ni hō-ō, "Paullownia and Phœnix," counts 20.

If a player gets eighty-eight points, he neither wins nor loses. Gains and losses are counted from this number, so much above or so much below.

This game is actually played by three persons, but the cards may be dealt to six, but usually to not less than three. The dealer is called *Oya* (literally, " parent "), the player on the right *Tsugi*[1] (" next," " succeeding "), and the third player *Biki* (a colloquial expression meaning " last "). The dealer is first determined by dealing two cards to each player, the one getting the highest count becoming *Oya*. In succeeding games, the last winner becomes *Oya* and the next last winner cuts the cards. Four cards are dealt from the top of the pack to the player on his right and so on, four to each, including the dealer, who then lays three cards face up on the mat. Three cards are then dealt in the same way to each player, and three placed face up on the table. The dealer plays first. He lays out a card, endeavoring to take one of the same suit on the table. If it matches he wins both cards and lays them aside, and they count at the end of the game. If he cannot take a card, the card he has played remains on the table. In either event, he draws another card from the pack and puts it down, winning with it any one it matches. The game is then continued around until the hand is played out.

In addition to the points counted for cards taken in playing, the following combinations of cards count as *Yaku* or prizes. They may be formed by cards first dealt or by combinations of the cards held in the hand with those taken, as specified below, and are announced by the player as soon as he obtains them, but without showing his cards. The *Yaku* count as so many *kwan* (Chinese, *kün*), a word meaning a string of 1,000 cash, but signifying in the game twelve points. These *Yaku* are as follows:

1. The four cards *Matsu ni tsuru, Sakura ni maku, Susuki ni tsuki,*[2] and *Kiri ni hō-ō*, called *Shiko* (" four shining ones "), count *hachi kwan* (eight *kwan*) = 96.

2. The three *Tanzaku* of the suits of *Matsu, Ume*, and *Sakura*, called *Urasu* (*matsu, ume, sakura*), count *go kwan* (five *kwan*) = 60.

3. The three blue *Tanzaku* (*Botan, Kiku*, and *Momiji*), called *Awotan* (blue *Tanzaku*), counts *go kwan* = 60.

The three preceding *Yaku* are called *Deki yaku*, or " Perfected *Yaku*." They must be formed by combining cards first dealt with cards drawn or entirely of cards drawn. The remaining *Yaku*, from 4 to 15, must be formed entirely from cards originally dealt, and are called *Te yaku*, or " Hand *Yaku*."

---

[1] Usually called *Doni*.

[2] This card is vulgarly called *bozu*, " priest," from its resemblance, it is said, to his shiny shaven crown.

9

4. Three cards of the same suit and a red *Tanzaku*, called *San bon*, counts *ichi kwan* (one *kwan*)=12.

5. More than two *Tanzaku*, either red or blue, and all other cards of one point, called *Aka* ("red"), counts *ichi kwan*=12.

6. One *Tanzaku* and all other cards of one point, called *Tan ichi* (*tanzaku* and "ones"), counts *ni kwan* (two *kwan*)=24.

The cards of the *Ame* suit all count as "ones" in making this *Yaku*.

7. One of the four cards, *Matsu ni tsuru*, *Sakura ni maku*, *Susuki ni tsuki*, and *Kiri ni hō-hō*, and all other cards of one point, called *Hikari ichi* ("shiners and ones"), counts *ni kwan*=24.

8. One card of ten points and all others one point, called *to ichi* ("ten and ones"), counts *ni kwan*=24.

9. Two cards of each of three suits, called *Kuttsuki* ("united"), counts *san kwan* (three *kwan*)=36.

10. Seven cards of one point, called *Karasu* ("empty"), counts *san kwan*=36.

11. Four cards of any suit, called *Te shi* ("hand four"), counts *shi kwan* (four *kwan*)=48.

12. Three cards of each of two suits, called *Roku san bon* ("six three cards"), counts *shi kwan*=48.

13. Three cards of one suit and two cards of each of two other suits, called *Hana ken*,[1] counts *go kwan*=60.

14. Two cards of one suit and four of any other suit, called *Ichi ni shi* ("one two, and four"), counts *roku kwan* (six *kwan*)=60.

15. Four cards of one suit and three of another, called *Shi-so* ("four and three"), counts *hichi kwan* (seven *kwan*)=84.

There are also double prizes, *Kasane yaku*, as when a player gets one of the four cards called *Hikari*, and six cards of one point, *Hikari ichi* (7), it counts two *kwan*, and if the hand also contains two cards of each of three suits, *Kuttsuki* (9), he wins three *kwan* for it in addition. If a player obtains either the *Aka*, *To ichi*, *Tan ichi*, or *Karasu*, and also gets more than 88 points by counting his cards, it is called *Nuke*, and he is entitled to count 12 points in addition.

If two players hold cards with which they should make *Nuke* and one inferior cards, and the former fail to gain 88 points while the latter achieves more than 88, he receives a prize of *ni kwan*, 24.

If, after playing, each gets more than 88 points, the *Oya*, or dealer, gets

---

[1] The meaning of this term was not known to my informants.

a prize of *hachi kwan*, 96. If one wins 146 points or more, it is called *Bai shō* ("two-fold prize"), and he is entitled to *hachi kwan*. If a player wins sixteen one-point cards, it is called *Su juroku* ("empty-sixteen"), and he receives *hachi kwan*. In this case the *Ame ni yanagi* may be counted as a one-point card.

When the cards are dealt a player may withdraw, but must pay a fine. This is called *nige*, "to run away." If he is *Oya*, he must pay two points; if he is *Tsugi*, four; and if *Biki*, six; but if there be one or more cards of 20 points on the table, the fine is doubled. If there be more than three players, the *Oya* will ask them in order whether they will play. This is called *oi-komi*, "to drive in." If a player then withdraws he will receive a prize of *han kwan* (½ *kwan*)=5, provided there be a blue *Tanzaku* among his cards.

The rules for playing which are given in this account are taken from a small illustrated handbook entitled *Hana garuta shi yō hō*, or "Rules for Playing Flower Cards," by Tamon Mayeda, published in Osaka in 1889.

The above-described game is called *Hachi ju-hachi*, or Eighty-eight, and is said to be a new game, and to have originated about forty years ago. The other common games are called *Yaku-bana* (*hana*) and *Towashi*.

Another kind of Japanese playing-cards are called *Mekuri fuda*, which are used in playing a game called *Mekuri*.[1] The pack comprises forty-eight cards, which, although much modified, may still be recognized as having been copied from the Spanish or Portuguese cards introduced into Japan in the sixteenth century. These cards are described in the *Wa Kan san sai dzu e* as the kind which were used in Japan at the time of its publication (A. D. 1712). They appear to have already departed from their original form. The encyclopedia states that the tenth card (the *Sota*), bears the picture of a priest; the eleventh (the *Caballo*), a horseman; and the twelfth (*El Rey*), a general.

Among other Japanese cards are the *Iroha-garuta*, or "Syllabary cards," which are used by children. These also consist of forty-eight cards, half of which bear a picture and one of the characters of the *Iroha*, or Japanese syllabary. Each of the other cards is inscribed with a proverb, the first word of which begins with one of the characters of the syllabary. There are several methods of play, the commonest being that of laying out all the picture-cards face up. A third person reads the proverbs to the players, who endeavor to select the cards with the corresponding initial from the table.

---

[1] Hepburn gives *tá má*, "playing horse," as the Chinese equivalent for *mekuri*.

The *Uta-garuta*, or "Poem cards," are played in the same manner as the preceding,[1] the game being called, according to Hepburn, *Uta-awase*, or "Poem-matching." They contain, according to Mr. Karl Himly, either the well-known one hundred poems, *Hyaku Nin Isshu*,[2] or poems of the "Ancient and Modern Collection," *Ko Kon Shū*. The picture cards bear a picture of the poet with the first two lines of the poems. The remaining lines are on the corresponding cards. A set comprises two hundred cards, one hundred of each kind. Before the Revolution (1868) Japanese children played with cards bearing Chinese poems called *Shikaruta*.

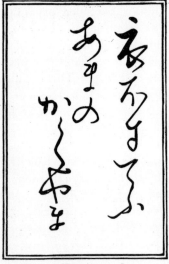

FIG. 124.—UTA-GARUTA. JAPAN.
(ACTUAL SIZE.)

A great variety of playing-cards are current in China. They are distinguished by a variety of symbols, and are remarkable for their shape, being usually very narrow in proportion to their length. The paper cards vary in size, quality, and color. Their width is from seven-sixteenths of an inch to one and one-half inches, and their length from two and three-eighths to four and three-quarters inches. They are either rectangular or have rounded corners. The backs are either plain white, black, red, orange, or blue, or bear printed designs in diaper and other patterns. In some packs the individual cards are distinguished by peculiarities in the ends of the printed border of the faces, by means of which they may be recognized when held in the hand in play.

The very complete collection of Chinese cards now in the Museum of the University of Pennsylvania was made by Mr. W. H. Wilkinson, and was exhibited by him in the collection of games shown by the writer at the

---

[1] Two or four persons usually play, although any number may take part. When two play, each takes fifty cards with the last lines at random, which he arranges, face up, before him. Each endeavors to touch first the corresponding cards, when the proverbs are read, and when a player first touches one on his opponent's side, he gives him three of his cards. The one who first disposes of all his cards wins the game.

[2] Translated by F. V. Dickens, *Japanese Lyrical Odes*, London, 1866. Each of the hundred poems is by a different poet.

World's Columbian Exposition at Chicago. These cards are classified by him, according to their symbols and marks, as follows :[1]

1. From the sapeck, or "cash," and its multiples.
2. Through Dominoes.
3. From *Tséung k'i*, the Chinese form of Chess.
4. From other sources.

I. CARDS DERIVED FROM MONEY OR MONEY TOKENS.

In Mr. Wilkinson's collection this class includes:
a. Kwan p'ái, "Stick cards," or, *Má tséuk*, "Hempen birds."
b. Lüt chi, "Waste paper."
c. Chung fát, "Hit and go."

a. KWAN P'ÁI.[2]

The simplest form of a *Kwan p'ái* pack consists of thirty cards, viz.: the ace, 2, 3, 4, 5, 6, 7, 8, and 9 in three suits, together with three court cards. The suits are (1) *ts'in*, "sapecks," or *ping*, "cakes;" (2) *sok*, "strings," or *kún*, "rouleaux;" (3) *mán*, "myriads." The court cards are usually *Hung fá*, "Red Flower;" *Pák fá*, "White Flower," and *Ts'in mán*, "Thousand Myriads," the last being popularly described as *Lò ts'in*, or "Old Thousand."

Kwan p'ái are, however, very rarely put up in this simple form. As a rule, four of these packs, or packets, of thirty cards go together, and with them are often provided in addition a number—two, five, or six, usually five, special cards, called by the Chinese *Kam*, or "Golds." These "Golds" play the same part as the old Mistigris, or the Joker in Euchre ; that is, they can take the place of any required card.

No. 1.—From Nanking. Four packets of thirty cards and five jokers. Index marks for suits and pips and for White Flower, Old Thousand, and each joker. The jokers are the Five Virtues: *yan, i, lai, chi, sun*—"humanity," "benevolence," "courtesy," "knowledge," and "sincerity." Total, 125.

No. 2.—From Peking. Four packets of thirty cards and six jokers. Described as *Wai p'ái—i. e.,* "cards from the cantonment" of Tientsin. Index

---

[1] The catalogue that follows, prepared by Mr. Wilkinson, was printed in the *Descriptive Catalogue, World's Columbian Exhibition, Department M. Revised Edition*, p. 84, Chicago, 1893. The original transliteration of the Chinese has been modified to agree with the Cantonese dialect used in this book.

[2] For a description of the methods in which *Kwan p'ái* are used in play, see *The Game of Khanhoo*, London, Chas. Goodall & Son, 1891.

marks for suits and pips and for White Flower, Red Flower, and two of the six jokers. The jokers are *Shí Ts'in, Wong Tò, Chiú K'oi, Ts'ing Shé, Pák Shé* and *Hü Sin*. These, which were put up outside the pack, are the heroes and heroines of certain tales. The first is a character in the Shwui Hú Chuen[1] (Water's Marge), a Robin Hood romance which furnishes names for the figures in the suit of myriads. The last three—"Blue Snake," "White Snake," and "Fairy *Hü*"—are taken from "The Tale of the White Snake." Total, 126.

No. 3.—From Hankow. Four packets of thirty each and five jokers. Index marks for suits and pips and for the coat cards. The jokers are the Five Blessings, viz.: *fuk*, "happiness;" *luk*, "promotion;" *shau*, "long life;" *hi*, "joy" (*i. e.*, "posterity"), and *ts'oi*, "wealth." The set was described on the original paper box in which it was sold as *Kam kwan*, "Golden *kwan*" (stick) cards. There are only three specimens of Old Thousand and of *Lam Ch'ung*, "White Flower." It is not unusual to find apparent defects of this kind in Western China packs. Total, 123.

No. 4.—From Hongkong. Four packets of thirty each and five jokers—the Five Blessings. No index marks. The wrapper was inscribed "Five Stars" (*i. e.*, the Five Jokers), and "Please note the real article, made by *Li* at the sign of *Mau* (luxuriance)." Total, 125

No. 5 —From Chungch'ing. Four packets of thirty each and five jokers, the Five Blessings, these last elaborately colored. Index marks as in No. 3, with slight modifications for *Wong Ying*, "Red Flower." Total, 125. Fig. 125.[2]

No. 6.—From Kiu Kiang. Four packets of thirty and five jokers— the Five Blessings. Described on wrapper as *ts'in, kún, sok*, "cash, rouleaux, and strings." Black backs, clipped corners; index marks for suits and pips. Maker's name, *Tsang*, on every card; his shop sign on Ace of cakes. Gilt marks on the Aces, the three coat cards, and the five jokers; red splashes on the 9's. Total, 125. Fig. 126.

No. 7.—From Fuhchau. Four packets of thirty; no jokers. Index

---

[1] Wylie's *Notes on Chinese Literature*, p. 162. Translated in part by M. Bazin, *Le Siècle des Youën*, Paris, 1850, p. 108.

[2] The pictures of Chinese playing-cards, with the exception of No. 126, are reproduced from Mr. Wilkinson's paper on the *Chinese Origin of Playing-Cards* in *The American Anthropologist*, for January, 1895, with the courteous permission of its editor. The coloring of the cards is represented by heraldic symbolism, the dotted signifying yellow or gold; vertical lines; oblique, green; horizontal, blue.

marks for pips and suits. Maker's sign, *Tái-lí*, on Aces and coat cards. Diapered backs. Total, 120.

No. 8.—From Peking. Four packets of thirty; no jokers. Index marks vary for suit and pips. Artistic cards in cream white on a black ground. Total, 120.

No. 9.—From Taiyuan, Shansi. Four packets of thirty; no jokers. Index marks for pips only. Designs very conventional. Total, 120.

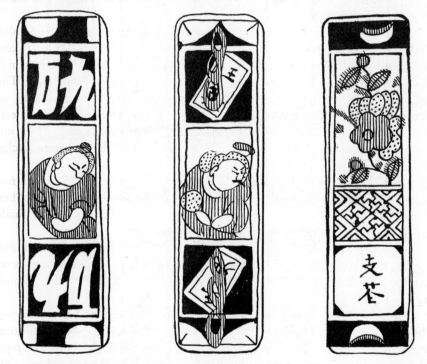

FIG. 125.—NINE OF MYRIADS, RED FLOWER AND WHITE FLOWER. CHUNGCH'ING. No. 5. (ACTUAL SIZE.)

No. 10.—From Wenchow. Two packets of thirty; no jokers. Index marks for suits and pips coarsely executed. Total, 60.

No. 11.—From Honan Province. Four packets of thirty; no jokers. Index marks for suits and pips. Names of each personage in the suit of myriads. Total, 120.

No. 12.—From Hongkong. Four packets of thirty; no jokers. No index marks. Total, 120.

No. 13.—From Canton. Originally put in a set of ten packets of thirty each; no jokers. Similar to No. 14. Total, in collection, 60.

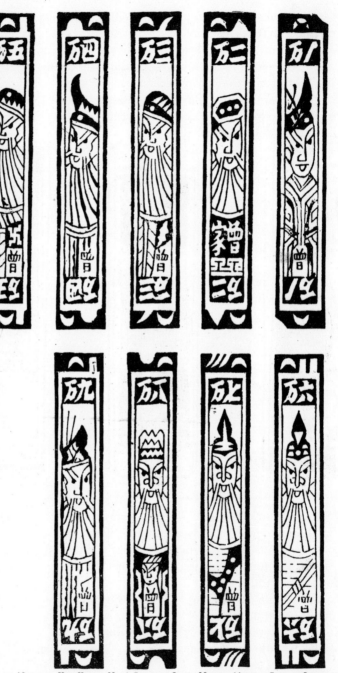

FIG. 126.—SUIT OF MYRIADS, KIU KIANG, No. 6, SHOWING INDEX MARKS. (ACTUAL SIZE OF IMPRESSIONS.)

No. 14.—From Hongkong. Four packets of thirty; no jokers; no index marks. Orange-colored backs. Total, 120. Fig. 127.

No. 15.—From Anhui Province. Five packets of thirty each, and five jokers—the Five Blessings. In the following cases two of the five are colored, three are plain: In each suit. 1, 2, 5, 8, 9; Old Thousand, *Wong Ying*, White Flower; jokers, Posterity and Wealth (total different cards, 10). Index marks for pips, suits, coat cards, and jokers. When the cards are colored, these index marks are for myriads and cakes in gold; for strings and jokers, in gold and red; when the cards are plain, the index marks are in white, except for nine of cakes (in red and white), and the coat cards. Diapered backs. Total, 155. Fig. 128.

No. 16.—From Hankow. Four packets of twenty-seven each; no coat cards or jokers. Index marks for suits and pips. Total, 108.

No. 17.—From Yü-tz'ŭ, near Taiyuan, Shansi. Four packets of thirty each; no jokers. Index marks for pips only. Designs very conventional. Total, 120.

b. LÜT CHI.

A *Lüt chi* pack is distinguished from a *Kwan p'ái*, (*a*) in that it is used for games in which the cards do not take one another; (*b*) from possessing four suits instead of three. These suits are (1) cash, (2) strings, (3) rouleaux, (4) lakhs. There are besides certain other cards which in play are reckoned as belonging to the suits of cash and lakhs respectively.

FIG. 127.—NINE OF MYRIADS. HONGKONG. No. 14. (ACTUAL SIZE.)

No. 22.—From Swatow. Ace to 9 of strings and rouleaux, 2 to 9 of cash and lakhs, and *Wan ts'in* (=Ace of cash); *Luk Fá*, "Stag Flower;" *Mò Kung*, "Prince of Mò," and *Pák Tsz'*, "Hundred Sons." The red impress consists of twelve characters, reading *Lung yap Liú kà pò fung, Kon kí ká chéung tai chéung*, "Town of *Lung* (Dragon), *Liú* family, *Pò Fung* (precious abundance). Sign of *Kon*, extra long, large cards." It is struck

FIG. 128.—THE FIVE BLESSINGS. ANHUI PROVINCE. No. 15. (½.)

on Hundred Sons, Prince of Mò, Ace of Cash, the four 9's and the 8 of lakhs. Total, 38.

No. 23.—From Canton. Similar to No. 22, but having in addition *Ts'in Tsz'* and *Mán Tsz'*, "Thousand Sons" and "Myriad Sons." The red impress reads, *Tsé ká Wing Fung chái, Yan ki ts'in kún sok.* "*Tsé* family, *Wing Fung* ('brilliant abundance') studio. Sign of *Yan* ('benevolence'). Cash, rouleaux, and strings." It is impressed on 9 of "strings," the 8, 9 of lakhs, 9 of rouleaux, Prince of Mò, Hundred Sons, Thousand Sons, Myriad Sons. Total, 40.

c. CHUNG FÁT.

As *Lüt chi* is confined to the Hakka country of South China, so is *Chung fát* to the provinces of Chekiang and Kiangsu. It is usually, if not invariably, put up in tablet rather than pasteboard form. The method of play is analogous to "*Khanhoo.*"

No. 43.—From Ningpo. Ace, 2, 3, 4, 5, 6, 7, 8, 9, of cash, strings, and myriads, quadrupled, four each of the cards marked East, West, North, South, *chung* and *fát* and eight blanks. Tablets of bone with bamboo backs. The coloring, whether in red, green, or blue, is purely ornamental and has nothing to do with the play of the game.

2. CARDS DERIVED FROM DICE AND DOMINOES.

The Chinese themselves make no great distinction between dice, dominoes, and domino-cards, styling them all *p'ái.* A set of Chinese dice usually consists of six, although it may contain three. The four spot is invariably colored red, the ace usually so; and this peculiarity is copied into all Chinese domino-cards. In these last the double-six, the best card in the pack, is very often colored partly red and partly black. "Cards" of this class appear indifferently in pasteboard and tablet form. The specimen packs in this collection may be divided as follows:

    a. T'in kau, "Heavens and nines."
    b. Fá ho, "Flower Harmony."
    c. Fá ho, variety.
    d. Eight *T'in kau.*
    e. Twelve *T'in kau.*
    f. Ün p'ái.
    g. Tong kau, or *Fá Tong kau.*

a. T'IN KAU.

The greatest possible number of combinations of a pair of dice is twenty-one. Each of these has in Chinese its name, and while eleven of the twenty-one are styled *man*, "civilian," the remaining ten are called *mó*, "military." Double the eleven civilian and add a set of military and the result is the thirty-two cards or dominoes of the game of *T'in kau*, a game which was certainly played in its present form in 1120 A. D., and is now popular all over the Chinese empire. It is remarkable that although of tablet form, the "cards" in this game invariably take one another.

No. 40.—From Shanghai. Bone with black wood backs.

No. 41.—From Canton. Bone with bamboo backs.

If from a *T'in kau* pack the following cards are rejected, viz., 4–5, 3–5, 2–4, 3–4, 2–5, 2–3, 1–4, 1–2, then with the remaining twenty-four a game very closely resembling the ordinary European game of Dominoes is played. At Wenchow the game is called *Chi lung*, "Connect the dragon."

b. FÁ HO, FLOWER HARMONY.

The game consists of twenty-one *T in kau* cards (1) plain, (2) illuminated, (3) doubled, three each of the first, two of the second, and one only of the third. There are thus sixty-three plain, forty-two illuminated, and twenty-one doubled, or 126 cards in all, together with a varying number of blanks serving the purpose of jokers. The game is played on the "Kan-hoo" principle, with, of course, certain differences.

No. 26.—From Shanghai. Known as "Actors' cards." The "illuminated" cards bear portraits of the heroes and heroines of certain plays, the "doubled" cards are duplicates of the "plain." The three jokers are "illuminated" cards without domino points. Total, 129. Fig. 129.

No. 45.—From Shanghai. A tablet set. The illuminated show sprays of flowers; the doubled, flowers and symbolic ornaments. The jokers, six in number, are blanks.

No. 24.—From Hankow. Known as *Fá-wong*, "Flower princes" (see No. 38). The twenty-one natural dominoes; three each plain, two each with flowers or ornamental objects, one each with a figure of a hero or heroine. No jokers. Total, 126.

No. 38.—From Hankow. Also a *Fá-wong*. The 126 cards as in No. 24. Illuminated cards have the *t'ái kik* (protyle dividing into the *yéung*, or male, and *yam*, or female, elements) in black and a black border; the doubles bear in red the hieroglyph *wong*, "prince" and have a black border.

c. VARIETY OF FÁ HO.

No. 30.—From Chungch'ing (Chungking) Known as *Fá p'ái*, or "Flower cards." Three each of the twenty-one natural dominoes plain, and four each illuminated. The illumination is a spray of flowers, and is the same for each card. Total, 147. It is to be noted that all Chungking domino packs are usually put up in the order of the dominoes, viz.: 6–6, 1–1, 4–4, 1–3 (3–3, 5–5 *sic*) 2–2, 5–6, 4–6, 1–6, 1–5 ; 3–6, 4–5, 2–6, 3–5, 2–5, 3–4, 2–3, 1–4, 2–4, 1–2.

d. PÁT T'IN KAU, OR EIGHT T'IN KAU.[1]

No. 27.—From Hankow. The twenty-one natural dominoes simply quintupled.

FIG. 129.—ACTORS' CARDS. SHANGHAI. No. 26. (ACTUAL SIZE.)

No. 28.—From Macao. Described on wrapper as *Tim p'ái*, or "Dotted cards." The twenty-one natural dominoes quintupled.

No. 31.—From Chungking. Known as *Ts'at hung p'ái*, or "Seven red cards." The twenty-one natural dominoes quintupled, one of each being illuminated. Of the 2–5 there is one extra card, but no illuminated. Total, 127. This game is played by the Chungking women, and is only in form a variety of *Fá ho*.

---

[1] This game is said to be of Cantonese origin Although packs are found as far west as Chungking, they are described as "Cantonese cards," and are kept in stock for sale to Cantonese residents.

e. SHAP-I T'IN KAU, OR TWELVE T'IN KAU.

No. 25.—From Hankow. The twenty-one natural quintupled, and these five cards: 1–3 2–3 1–2, 1–5 3–6 2–4, 3–5 1–4 2–6, 3–4 1–6 2–5, 4–5 5–6 4–6. These are known as *Sam*, or "Hearts."

f. ÜN PÁI.

Under 2*a* (*T'in kau*) the game of *Chi lung*, or Dominoes, was described as played with a *T'in kau* pack from which the following eight cards had been thrown out, viz.: 4–5, 3–5, 2–4, 3–4, 2–5, 2–3, 1–4, 1–2. The twenty-four cards left will be described as a *Chi lung* pack.

No. 34.—From Shansi province. The card 1–4 being substituted for 1–3, this consists of a double *Chi lung* pack. Total, 48.

No. 37.—From Chungch'ing. Somewhat similar to No. 34, except that the cards 1–2 and 3–4 are substituted for the two 1–3's. One of each of the fourteen kinds is illuminated. Total, 48.

g. TONG KAU.

No. 44.—From Wenchow. The twenty-one natural dominoes quintupled, and the following seventeen special cards: (1) 6–6 6–3, (2) 1–1 1–3, (3) 4–4 1–3, (4) 2–4 4–4, (5) 3–3 5–6, (6) 1–2 2–2, (7) 1–2 2–4, (8) 4–5 5–5, (9), (10), (11), the sequence 1–6, (*a*) *man*, "civilian;" (*b*) *mò*, "military;" (*c*) *tsung*, "universal;" (*d*) *t'oi*, "highness;" (*e*) *ho*, "lily;" (*f*) *p'ui*, "heap up." The blanks are used only to replace cards lost. The coloring of the cards is immaterial. Total, 122.

The pack as above is known as *Fá Tong kau*, "Flowery *Tong kau*." The simpler form, or *Tong kau* proper, has only five special cards, viz.: 6–6 6–3, 1–1 1–3, 4–4 1–3, 6–6 3–3, 1–2 2–4. It is usually put up with two blanks.

3. CARDS DERIVED FROM TSEUNG K'I, THE CHINESE CHESS.

These seem to be peculiar to the Southern and Southeastern provinces, notably Fuhkien and Kwangtung.

No. 18.—From Swatow. Eight each of the seven black and of the seven white men, except that of the soldiers, there are ten of each color. The Generals (Kings) are elaborately ornamented. Long, narrow gray cards, apt to curl up. Total, 116. This, in common with all other packs of its class, is known as *Kü-má-p'áu*, "Rook-knight-cannon."

No. 19.—From Fuhchau. Four each of the red and the same number of the black cards. Remarkable for having index marks. Elaborate patterns on backs. Total, 56.[1]

No. 20.—From Swatow. Four each of the *Tséung, Sz', Tséung, Kü, Má, P'áu* in red, the same number in black, and ten each of the red and of black pawns, one black and one red *kam*, "gold" or joker. Total, 70. The pack comes from Lung-chou, near Hui-chou, some fifty miles from Swatow.

No. 21.—From Swatow. Four each of the seven kinds in four colors — red, yellow, white, green.

The firm name, *Lí Shing*, is on the red and yellow Kings, *Lí* on all the other yellows and reds, *Shing* on all the greens and whites. Total, 112.

No. 29.—From Canton. Four each of the seven men in four colors: red, yellow; white, green, and five jokers, the Five Blessings. The jokers in this example are printed on white; they are sometimes met with in red. Total, 117.

4. MISCELLANEOUS CARDS.

This class of cards, drawn in the present collection entirely from Western China, bears some resemblance to the " Proverbs " and " Happy Families," of Europe and America. With the exception, however, of the *Wá-wá p'ái*, or children's cards, these Chinese packs are used by adults, and may be legitimately included in a collection of Chinese cards.

a. CARDS BASED ON NUMBERS.

No. 33.—From Chungch'ing. The first ten natural numbers (*a*) in large script, (*b*) in small script, four of each. Of each number, one card bears a scene from a play, the remaining three cards have one, or sometimes two, branches of flowers, in red. The numbers II, VII, X, 2, 7, 10, are printed in red with a spray of peony blossom; the rest are in black, I, III, IV, V with a single bunch, VI, VIII, IX with a double branch, of flowers, I, 3, 4, 5, 6, 8, 9 all with a double bunch. Total, 80.

No. 39.—From Hankow. Four each of the first ten natural numbers, (*a*) in large script, (*b*) in small script, and the following eight special cards: (1) 2 | 7 | 10, red; (2) II | VII | X, red; (3) 3 | 6 | 9, black; (4) III | VI | IX, black; (5) a crab, black; (6) a butterfly or bat, red; (7) *hong*, "descend," black; (8) *shing*, "ascend," red. All the cards are hand-painted. The crab and butterfly serve the purposes of jokers. Total, 48.

---

[1] A card-holder, made of pewter, accompanies this pack, intended to obviate any advantage derivable from marked backs. In it, after dealing the ten cards to each of the two, three, or four players, the stock is placed; the bottom card is then drawn.

b. CARDS BASED ON A WRITING LESSON.

The earliest, or one of the earliest writing lessons set to a Chinese child, commences *Shéung tái yan,* "*Once* (there was a) great man." There are several variants of the lessons, which in Hunan province and other parts of Western China forms the basis of the most popular card parks.

No. 35.—From Hankow. The screed runs: *Shéung tái yan | yau üt ki fá sám ts'in | ts'at shap sz' | Ni siú shang | pát kau tsz' | ho chi lai | i sz' 'ng luk.* That is, " Once a great man *Yau Üt-ki* (Confucius) converted three thousand, seventy were disciples ; you small scholars, eight or nine youths, may learn politeness ; two, four five, six." Each of these twenty-one hieroglyphs, except *ho,* " may," of which there are only four, is quintupled. Total, 124.

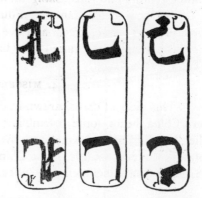

No. 36.—From Hankow, but like No. 35, really from Hunan province.

Similar to No. 35, but (*a*) for *Yau* is substituted *Hung,* the surname of Confucius, and for *ho chi lai | i sz' 'ng luk,* are employed *kái tsok yan | fuk luk shau,* " gratefully practice humanity ; happiness, promotion, longevity ;" (*b*) there are

FIG. 130.—CARDS WITH WRITING LESSON. HAN-KOW. No. 36. (½.)

only four of each kind, not five. All handwritten on smooth oiled paper. The first card of each triplet is in red, the other two are in black. The second card has a red mark at the top and bottom. The cards have index marks, a miniature hieroglyph at the right-hand corner of each. Total, 96. Fig. 130.

c. CARDS BASED ON LUCKY FORMULA.

No. 32.—From Chungch'ing. The *Wá-wá p'ái,* or children's cards. Eight cards each of the hieroglyphs, *Fuk ü tung hoi | shau pi nám shán,* " Happiness, like the eastern sea, age more than the southern hills." The eight *fuk* and the eight *shau* are in red ; the rest in black ; one *fuk* has upon it a spray of flowers. Total, 64. Fig. 131.

The playing-cards sold in the Chinese shops in the United States are similar to Nos. 13 and 14 in Mr. Wilkinson's collection. They are usually put up in small pasteboard boxes, containing four packets of thirty cards. The backs of these cards are usually red or black, and sometimes white. They are commonly known as *Tséung kwan chí p'ái,* or "Commander-in-chief cards."

Although generally sold in their shops, these cards are seldom, if ever, used by the Chinese in the United States for the purpose of play, and comparatively few of the immigrants understand the card games, the long wooden dominoes described on page 116 taking the place of cards. Playing-cards are used, however, as counters or chips in the game of *Fán t'án,*[1] for which purpose cards with plain white backs are used. Narrow cards with red backs are also used to register bets upon the board

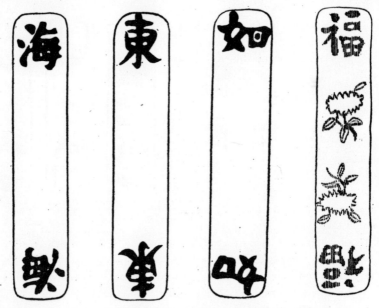

Fig. 131.—Children's Cards. Chungch'ing. No. 32. (⅔.)

in the same game, special cards having two red faces, without devices, called *káu lí,* or "dog tongues," being sold for the purpose. The *Tséung kwan chí p'ái* are regarded as a powerful charm to drive away evil spirits, and are placed upon the coffin when a dead body is transported from one place to another.

The *Tséung kwan chí p'ái* are sometimes spoken of as the *Sám shap luk t'in tséung ts'at shap i tí shát,* or the "Thirty-six heavenly Generals and seventy-two earthly malignants." They are also called the *Yat pák ling*

---

[1] Cf. *The Gambling Games of the Chinese in America.*

pát, or "One hundred and eight." Both of these names refer to the one hundred and eight heroes or personages of the Shwui Hú Chuen, whose pictures, often with their names appended and apparently copied from an illustrated edition of the novel, occur on the suit of *Mán*, or "myriads."

The origin of these cards appears to be directly traceable to the Korèan *Htou-tjyen*. The index-marks at the ends which are shown in the pack from Hankow, Fig. 126, and are practically identical on all the packs in Mr. Wilkinson's extensive collection from various parts of China, may be regarded as survivals of the cut-feather numerals of the Korean cards. The suits consist of numerical series from one to nine, the extra cards of the Chinese packs taking the place of the "General" cards of the Korean. Indeed, the latter may have furnished the name of "Commander in Chief," or "General," applied by the Cantonese to these packs.[1] The reduction in the number of suits from eight to six and even four, according to the number of players, occurs in the *Htou-tjyen*.

Another point of correspondence between the Chinese and Korean cards is found in the agreement between the name of the latter, *tsín*, with the money symbols, *ts'ín*, that occur on the Chinese money-cards. The addition of the money symbols to the *Htou-tjyen* seems most natural in view of the relation that appears to exist between the *tsín*, or written tablets of bamboo, and the *ts'ín*, or current money of China. The present form of the *Tséung kwan p'ái* is doubtless later than the novel, written by Shí Nái Ngán, in the Yuen dynasty (A. D. 1280–1368), from which the pictures on the higher cards were taken. In conclusion, it may be observed that the Korean *Htou-tjyen* may be regarded as survivals of the ancestral type, if not of the direct ancestors of existing Chinese cards, and that, as before mentioned, they may be directly traced to the arrow, in which they originated.

XCIII. SAN-HTONG—LOTTERY.

This agrees very closely with the *Kyei* (Chinese, *k'ai*), or money-lending clubs. The membership in these clubs may be 10, 20, 50, 100, or 1,000, but is usually 50 or 100. The members each contribute the same amount at fixed intervals, and a drawing takes place at the same time, at which the entire amount contributed is drawn by one of the members, and this is continued until each have got back their own. The drawing is conducted with wooden balls about the size of marbles, for which hazel nuts

---

[1] Mr. Wilkinson describes these cards as "stick" cards, the word stick, *kwan*, having the same sound as *kwan* in *tséung kwan*.

are frequently used. These are marked in Chinese characters with the names and numbers of the members, and are put in an oval wooden box, which consists of two parts and opens in the middle, and has a mouth like that of a bottle, from which the balls are shaken. This box, called *San-htong* (Chinese, *ts'im t'ung*), meaning "tube for lots," gives its name to the lottery. The drawings are usually held every month, but not upon any special day. There are two ways in which the clubs are conducted. In one the player continues to pay, after he has been successful, until the end of the drawings. In the other, by agreeing to accept less than the amount actually won, he compounds for future payments, and withdraws. It is customary for the club to choose a member who manages its affairs, for which he receives a small commission. The club frequently has a little money which is put out at interest, and sometimes, when the entire hundred, or whatever number is agreed upon, cannot be made up, the club takes a sufficient number of shares to complete it. If a player is unable to pay, he may sell his share to the club. Poor merchants frequently help each other by this means.

The Chinese laborers in the United States have organized a lottery in most of their larger colonies, which appears to have originated directly from something like the Korean *San-htong*. In this lottery, called *Tsz' fá*, or " Word Blossoming," thirty-six names of men and women are used as lots. Any one may buy whichever name he chooses, and receives thirty times the amount of his stakes if he guesses the winning name. This lottery is complicated by the use of a chart called the *tsz' fá t'ò*, shown in Fig. 132, on which the thirty-six names are printed. They are divided into the following categories:

1. The four *Chong ün.*[1]
2. The seven successful merchants.
3. The four Buddhist priests.
4. The five beggars.
5. The five generals.
6. The four ladies.
7. The four destined to good fortune.
8. The nun.
9. The two Taoist priests.

Each of these names appear in a ruled division of the chart, which is

---

[1] The highest degree at the examinations for the Hanlin.

subdivided by horizontal lines into three parts. In the middle, below the name itself, are two names, one of them, in most cases, that of an animal, and the other that of some historical personage, while the lower division contains two characters which constitute the surname of one of the names that appear in the upper division. In the middle of the chart is the picture

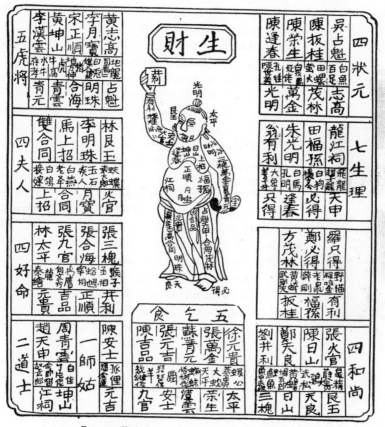

FIG. 132.—Tsz' fá t'o. Chart for Tsz' fá Lottery.
From original in the Museum of Archæology, Univ. of Penna. No. 7151.

of a man, who is known as the *T'ung Yan*, or " Composite man," over whom are written the thirty-six surnames before referred to. It is said that this chart, which is analogous to the dream books sold in the United States, serves the same purpose with the more ignorant gamblers among the Chinese laborers, the player betting upon the name written upon the part of the body of which he happened to dream, or, if he dreamed of an animal or some character in the historical novels, on the name which is given in connection which that animal or personage. This appears to have been the original purpose of the chart, but this employment is secondary to one in which superstition has less part. The writer of the lottery composes an original ode, called *t'ai*, "composition," for each day's drawings, which must contain, either directly or by implication, some demonstrable reference to one of the objects or persons mentioned in the middle space of the division in which the winning name occurs, or some reference to the part of the man's body upon which the name appears. The lottery's chances are increased by the writer being permitted to select as the winning name either the name in the upper space or its alternate in the lower space of each of the thirty-six divisions. The manager of the lottery hands each player a copy of the ode referring to the next day's drawings at the conclusion of each day's business.

The odes usually consist of two measured couplets, each composed of lines of three and five characters, printed in green or blue ink upon white paper. The first couplet on the right must contain a reference to the afternoon drawing, and the other to the one that takes place in the evening. The following is a specimen: Fig. 133.

FIG. 133.—TSZ' FÁ T'AI. ENIGMA FOR TSZ' FÁ LOTTERY.

Kwok yau tò,
Man man chim ü tò,
Kun ün yung,
Pak sing ch'eung wo fung.

"The country has the (right) way."
"All the people with rain and dew are moistened."
"The officers all forbear."
"The people spread abroad with favorable winds."

It is the practice of the writer of the lottery to mislead the players as far as possible by means of his verses, but he must always be able to give a satisfactory explanation of their connection with the name he displays.

The drawings are managed by rolling a piece of white paper, upon which the last two characters of the winning name are plainly written, within a piece of black cloth which is hung in the room where the drawing takes place. When the bets are all made, the manager slowly unrolls the cloth and reveals the winning name. This procedure probably explains the peculiar name, *Tsz' fá*, or "Word Blossoming," which is given to the game.[1]

There is another form of lottery which is even more popular than the preceding among the Chinese in the United States. It is popularly known as the *Pák kòp piú*, or "White Pigeon Ticket." Like the *Tsz' fá*, it is conducted by regularly organized companies who hold drawings once or twice daily. The tickets, which are imported already printed from China, invariably consist of pieces of paper about five inches square, upon which have been printed in black, blue, or green ink the first eighty characters of the *Ts'in Tsz' Man*, or "Thousand Character Classic." This book, which contains precisely one thousand characters, no two of which are alike, is so well known in China that its characters are frequently used instead of the corresponding numerals from one to one thousand. They serve the purpose of numbers on the tickets. The impression on these tickets is reproduced in Fig. 134. Twenty of the eighty numbers are drawn every night. The company sells the players ten or more numbers and pays prizes to those who guess the characters drawn. A player prepares his tickets by dotting the character he selects with black ink, and this ticket is handed to the manager with the money wagered. Eighty pieces of white paper are provided at the drawing, upon which have been written or printed the eighty characters on the tickets, one on each, a box of hand stamps for the purpose forming part of the equipment of most lotteries. The manager rolls the eighty pieces of paper into as many pellets, so that they cannot be distinguished, one from another, and places them in a large tin pan. He mixes them thoroughly and, then, one at a time counts twenty of the pellets into a white china bowl, distinguished by a paper label marked "one." He then counts twenty more into another bowl marked "two," and, in turn places the remainder in two other bowls marked "three" and "four." One of the players, who is paid a small gratuity, is now asked to select one of

---

[1] Archdeacon Gray describes this lottery as being played in China under the name of "Koo-yan," or "the Ancients," and says it is also known as "Flowery Characters." The names of the animals associated with the names and surnames are explained by him as those of the forms of being in which the several personages existed in a former state of existence. He states that this game originated in the department of Chun-chow and was introduced into Canton in the twenty-eighth year of Taou-kwang (A. D. 1848).

the bowls, and the one he designates is declared to contain the winning numbers. These the manager carefully unrolls, one at a time, at once pasting them upon a board in the back part of the office.

Those who purchase ten numbers lose their stakes unless they happen to have bought at least five of the winning numbers. Those who guess

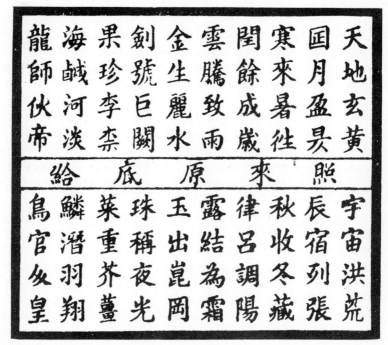

FIG. 134.—TICKET FOR PÁK KOP PIU LOTTERY. KWANGTUNG, CHINA, AND CHINESE IN THE UNITED STATES.

five or more of the winning numbers receive the following sums for each dollar they wager.

For 5 winning numbers,	. . . .	$2.00
" 6 " "	. . . .	20.00
" 7 " "	. . . .	200.00
" 8 " "	. . . .	1,000.00
" 9 " "	. . . .	1,500.00
" 10 " "	. . . .	3,000.00

The companies, however, always deduct five per cent. from these amounts, and when the ticket has been sold through an agent, fifteen per cent., ten per cent. of which is paid to the agent. Proportional sums are paid when the amount wagered is less than one dollar.

Most of the companies sell more than ten numbers, from ten up to twenty, at a proportional advance in prices as the player's chances are increased. The price which should be charged for more than ten numbers, with the prizes to be paid, and the methods of calculating the company's chances, and what its profits should be, are contained in a book known as the *Pák Kòp Piú T'ò*, of which several editions are current among the gamblers in American cities. One in general use, entitled, *Shang Ts'oi Tsit King*, or "Quick Way to Get Rich," may be purchased in Chinese shops.[1]

The name of this game, *pák kòp piú* appears to the writer to be a corruption of *pak hòp piú*, or "One Hundred United Lottery." If this be true, its resemblance to the Korean *San-htong* is still further increased.

It is customary for the Chinese in the United States to resort to a shrine of Kwan Ti, the God of War, the divinity generally worshiped by the Chinese in America, before playing this game. Here is kept a set of bamboo lots, *ts'im* (Korean, *sān*), marked with the eighty numbers of the lottery tickets. The intending player, after performing the customary rites, kneels and shakes these lots from their receptacle, a bamboo box or tube about eighteen inches in length called *ts'im t'ung*, in order to divine the lots which will be lucky at play. It will be observed that this ceremonial procedure is similar to that now employed in Korea in actual gambling, and that the name of the implement employed, *ts'im t'ung* (Korean, *san-htong*), is identical.

立
月
卜
巳
三

龍

Fig. 135.-Syou-sou-kyet-ki. Enigma and Answer. Korea.

XCIV. SYOU-SOU-KYET-KI—ENIGMAS.

Although games are ordinarily forbidden to children in Korea, certain games of a literary character, as *Tjyong-kyeng-to* (LXXI), and others to be described, are permitted and even encouraged. Enigmas, *Syou-sou-kyet-ki*, are a common diversion, as for example: "What character would the characters *ip*, *ouel*, *hok*, *keui* and *sam* (Chinese, *lap*, *üt*, *puk*, *ki* and *sám*) make if joined together?" The answer is *ryong* (Chinese, *lung*) "dragon."

XCV. TJA-MAT-TCHIM—WORD TALLYING.

This is a literary game which children are always encouraged to play, and indeed, it sometimes forms one of their school exercises. Two, three, or

---

[1] Cf. *The Gambling Games of the Chinese in America.* By Stewart Culin, Philadelphia. 1891.

four play. When two play, one chooses *Ha-nal*, "Heaven," and the other *Ti*, "Earth." A Chinese book is then opened and the one who chooses "Heaven" examines the open page on the right, while the one who choose "Earth" examines the open page on the lower side on the left. They continue to examine the corresponding pages on the right and left in the book. The objects of their search are two or three identical characters arranged in the following ways: * *, *ka-ro-tja-mat-tchim*, or "crosswise word tallying;" ⁕ *mai-tol-tja-mat-tchim*, "pestle word tallying;" *et-kăi-tja-mat-tchim*, "shoulder word tallying;" *⁎, *ka-ro-tja-mat-tchim*, "oblique word tallying;" * * *, *san-tja-mat-tchim*, "three word tallying," and * ° * *noun-kal-tja-mat-tchim*, or "eye-ball word tallying. All of these combinations count one unless otherwise agreed. The players go over the book, page by page, and the one who gets the highest number, wins. When three or more play the book is not divided. Each player announces a *mat-tchim* as soon as he finds it, and it counts for him. If a player makes a mistake, as frequently happens, he loses all he has made, or a certain number, according to agreement.

XCVI. KOL-MO-TOM-HA-KI—DISTRICT PICKING.

This is another literary game. A Chinese book is opened as in the preceding game and each player endeavors to pick out as many names of Korean cities and towns as possible from the words on the exposed page, adding when necessary to form such names one of the Chinese characters which the Koreans call *san*, *tchyen*, *tjyou* and *syeng* (Chinese, *shán*, "mountain;" *ch'ün*, "mountain streams;" *chan*, "district," and *shing*, "city"), common geographical suffixes. Only Korean geographical names are taken, and sometimes, when geographical names are numerous in the book, the suffixes are not permitted. The same character may be used more than once, but not to form the same name. The one who finds the highest number wins, and the lowest must pay a treat.

A somewhat similar game is played by Japanese children under the name of *Ji tsunagi*. Two or more play. A simple Chinese character is agreed upon and each in turn, as the game goes around, endeavors to combine with the given radical some character which will form a compound. When a player is unable to do this he loses, and the game is continued until one remains the winner.

XCVII. TCHO-TJYOUNG-TJYANG.

This is also a literary game. The name (Chinese, *chung cheung chéung*) means literally "First, middle chapter." A Chinese book is opened at random, and each player endeavors to pick out a character which is the initial character in one of the Chinese classical odes. Sometimes they confine the selection to the first characters of the lines of a particular ode in the Book of Poetry. The one who finds such a character must repeat the line, and this may not be selected again. The one who gets the highest number wins. It is customary to write down the lines. There are many forms of this game.

INDEX TO KOREAN NAMES.

INDEX TO JAPANESE NAMES.

INDEX TO CHINESE NAMES.

The words in Roman are transliterated in the Cantonese dialect, and those in small capitals, chiefly proper names and titles, in the Northern dialect according to Williams.

164

GENERAL INDEX.